Scottish Mountaineering Club
District Guide Books

THE WESTERN HIGHLANDS

DISTRICT GUIDE BOOKS

Southern Highlands
Central Highlands
Western Highlands
Northern Highlands
Islands of Scotland
Island of Skye
The Cairngorms
Southern Uplands
Scottish Highlands

Munro's Tables

SCOTTISH MOUNTAINEERING CLUB
DISTRICT GUIDE BOOKS

THE
Western Highlands

by G. Scott Johnstone

THE SCOTTISH MOUNTAINEERING TRUST
EDINBURGH

First published in Great Britain in 1973 by
THE SCOTTISH MOUNTAINEERING TRUST

Copyright © 1973 by the Scottish Mountaineering Trust

First Edition 1931
Second Edition 1932
Third Edition 1947
Fourth Edition 1964
First Edition New Series 1973
Reprinted 1979

Designed for the Scottish Mountaineering Trust by
West Col Productions

TRADE DISTRIBUTORS
West Col Productions
Goring on Thames
Reading Berks RG8 9AA

SBN 901516 66 X

Set in Monotype Plantin Series 110 and Grotesque 215
Reproduced, printed and bound in Great Britain by
Fakenham Press Limited, Fakenham, Norfolk

CONTENTS

ILLUSTRATIONS

ILLUSTRATIONS

All photographs by the author except where indicated.

Illustrations numbers 6 and 7 are I.G.S. photographs reproduced by permission of the Director, Institute of Geological Sciences. Crown Copyright Reserved.

FOREWORD

THIS is the fifth edition of the Western Highlands District Guide Book and the area covered includes some of the wildest parts of the Highlands. The increasing efforts to attract tourists however has resulted in an improvement in the roads and easier access. This, and a revision of their maps by the Ordnance Survey resulting in a change in the recorded heights of a number of mountains, has required a checking of all the heights recorded in the Guide Book and the re-writing of most parts.

The S.M.C. were fortunate in retaining the services of Scott Johnstone, who has an unrivalled knowledge of the area, to undertake the task. He has also included in the Introduction a section on Geology, a subject on which he is fully qualified to write, explaining how the Highlands have been built up. He has given up much of his spare time in recent months to produce this Guide Book and the Club records its thanks.

W. B. Speirs, *Glasgow*, January 1973.

ACKNOWLEDGMENT

In the re-writing of this District Guide Book the author has made considerable use of the topographic details of the hills given in the former editions by J. A. Parker. It would have been difficult indeed to better his meticulous descriptions where these are applicable. The author is also much indebted to several friends and colleagues who have supplemented in detail his wider, but in places more superficial, knowledge of the area.

PROPRIETARY AND
SPORTING RIGHTS

THE Scottish Mountaineering Trust desire to impress upon all those who avail themselves of the information given in their Guide Books that it is essential to consider and respect proprietary and sporting rights.

During the shooting season, from about the beginning of August to the middle of October, harm can be done in deer forests and on grouse moors by people tramping through them. During this period walkers and climbers should obtain the consent of the local stalkers and gamekeepers before walking over shooting lands. At times it is not easy to recognize what constitutes shooting lands. In cases of doubt it is always wise to ask some local resident.

It should also be noted that many of the roads in the upper glens were made and are maintained by the proprietors, who do not acknowledge a public right to motor over them, though they may follow the lines of established rights-of-way. It is, however, frequently possible to obtain permission to motor over some of them, but, as the situation is liable to change, local enquiries should be made in advance.

INTRODUCTION

THE Western Highlands district is taken to be that part of Scotland north of the Great Glen but south of the through valley system defined by the Cromarty Firth, Strath Conon, Strath Bran and Strath-carron – the line, in fact, of the Dingwall–Kyle of Loch Alsh railway whose doubtful future at the time of writing prevents it being used as a useful geographical reference feature!

This area measures about 85 miles from north-east to south-west and has greatest width, at right angles to the Great Glen, of about 35 miles.

The western seaboard of the district is highly indented by long fiord-like sea lochs and inlets, with the result that although the direct line from Morvern to Loch Carron is only about 60 miles its coastline measures no less than 330 miles. In contrast the south-east boundary of the district – the Great Glen of Scotland – is an almost dead straight line from Morvern to Inverness. The geological reasons for these features will be discussed later.

The main watershed of Scotland lies well to the west of the area, more or less north-south from Glen Tarbert, with the result that many of the west-flowing rivers are short and steep, especially as nearly all reach sea level at the head of sea-lochs well inland from the open water of the Sea of the Hebrides or Sound of Sleat. North of Loch Arkaig, however, the easterly-trending valleys are long and gently-graded.

One very remarkable feature of the district is the sub-parallel system of west-east through valleys which traverse it from the western seaboard to the Great Glen. Reading from south to north these are Loch Sunart–Glen Tarbert, Loch Ailort–Loch Eilt–Loch Eil, Loch Morar–Loch Arkaig, Loch Nevis–Loch Quoich–Glen Garry (with its branch of Loch Hourn–Loch Quoich), Loch Duich–Glen Shiel–Glen Moriston, Loch Duich–Glen Lichd–Glen Affric, Loch Carron–Glen Cannich and the Loch Carron–Cromarty Firth system mentioned above. One could stretch a point and include the east-west Glen

Strathfarrar, Glen Orrin, and Strath Conon as well. As a result of this east-west dissection the country is naturally divided for the purposes of description into areas lying between the valleys and, with some local subdivision based on other natural features, it will be treated in this account on that basis. The method is also convenient because the main access to the hills is by way of public or private roads and paths which follow these valleys.

Neither in summer nor in winter does the district offer much to the rock-climber except on Garbh Bheinn of Ardgour, but to the less specialist mountaineer it has great attractions. In summer, because of the tendency of the mountains to lie in continuous chains on the valley divides, long days at high level can be had in many areas with the ridges in places being pleasantly narrow without being difficult. Many of the mountains in the west have really magnificent views along the deep western valleys out to the sea-lochs and the Hebrides, while in the same area the hillsides themselves are steep and very rocky. In winter excellent expeditions can be had along these ridges, many of which will then merit the use of proper mountaineering techniques, while the steep corrie walls commonly provide straightforward snow climbs. Unfortunately the steeper western mountains tend to loose their snow easily under the action of the westerly winds from the sea. East of the watershed snow conditions usually improve.

Indeed the variation of climate is remarkable. Looking west along the through valleys one often can see a grey wall of rain shutting off everything west of the watershed, but thinning out rapidly eastwards. One of the author's colleagues, who worked for several years in Glen Moriston, used to refer to this as the 'Cluanie Curtain' and the simile is most apt. The name has stuck and the surveyors now use it for the same phenomenon in any of the major valleys.

It must be admitted that the rainfall in the Western Highlands is pretty high. An average for nearly 40 years gives about 50 inches per year for Mallaig and the western coastline, rising eastwards with astonishing rapidity to figures of 125–170 inches over the watershed and falling off eastwards to the Great Glen, where figures of around 50 inches are once more obtained. Local areas on the watershed commonly have rainfall in excess of 170 inches.

Probably the wettest spot is the area around Sgurr na Ciche. At a rain gauge near what is now the Lochan na Cruadhach cut-off dam at the west end of the Quoich Reservoir a fall of 213·42 inches was recorded in 1938, of which 50·03 inches fell in March. In January

1916 about 44 inches fell while on 11 October 8·2 inches were recorded in twenty-four hours! Huddled under his cagoule in the passes on several wet occasions, the author is convinced that the record has been surpassed many times in the past twenty years, but unrecorded, although hard statistics state that in this period the maximum fall was 205 inches in 1961, also at the cut-off dam.

Of more general interest, however, is the overall weather pattern. In the southern half of the Western Highlands the author's Geological Survey colleagues kept approximate records for the months of May to August for about 5 years. Over the whole area one day in three had rainy, cloudy or otherwise unpleasantly damp weather for the hills. On the watershed hills it was estimated that one day in two was a realistic figure. Like any average this can be misleading. Long dry spells can, and do, occur. So can long wet ones. The author's record was August 1949 when practically no rain fell. One subsequent August had, literally, no dry days. On the whole August tends to be wet. May and June are the best months while January is often clear and cold but without much snow on the hills. Autumn weather at the end of October is sometimes delightful and as it is after the stalking season may be a good time to visit the hills. The good spells, unfortunately, cannot be relied on.

The hill country of course is all under sheep and deer. Climbers are not welcome in certain areas during the stalking season – generally August to mid-October – while there are several areas where landowners claim that the deer should not be disturbed for a greater or lesser period beforehand. It is impossible to give advice in detail concerning these problems and good sense and courtesy should prevail on both sides. In general it will be found that the later dates are workable. Fortunately they coincide with a bad weather risk and there is less difficulty in Winter or early Spring when the mountains are at their most attractive. One positive advantage of the sporting estates is that in their heyday access paths to passes and corries were constructed, at great cost in personal labour, all over the area. Most are shown on the one-inch Ordnance Survey maps.

Maps

The Western Highlands Guide Book is not meant to be self-contained and is based on the assumption that the reader, if studying the area in detail, will have access to good maps. As a result, while details are given for all the main peaks, subsidiary summits, say, on a ridge, are not detailed unless there is a special reason for doing so. The best map, of course, is the Ordnance Survey one-inch 7th Series, although the reader will find that for planning a holiday the Bartholomew's half-inch maps are very good, although in certain cases differing in spelling. Note that if the 7th Series O.S. map is referred to it should be the latest edition. The maps have been revised and some early ones do not show the post-war reservoir construction details.

Heights present a problem. In several cases heights of mountains have been changed, not only from those given on the former Popular Edition map, *but between successive printings of the 7th series map*. The heights quoted are from maps purchased in 1972. The only serious effect on Munro's Tables is mentioned in Chapter 10.

Spelling in the Guide follows the O.S., but the writer sees no advantage in sprinkling the text with the accented vowels. The remainder of the pronunciation will provide problems enough for the non-initiated! The accents have therefore been omitted except in the glossary at the end, where the reader can make what he likes of them.

The country is one where Naismith's Rule operates well. Times may be estimated with fair accuracy, on the basis of an average party, at one hour for three map miles plus half an hour for every 1000 ft. of ascent.

Accommodation

The view has been taken that most people visiting the Western Highlands will do so by car. Because of this the question of local accommodation is largely irrelevant as all the hills (with the exception of those of Knoydart) albeit with some effort, can be climbed using car transport from one or other of the major communities. These are Fort William, Fort Augustus, Inverness, Mallaig, Dornie or Kyle of Lochalsh, depending on the general area to be visited. Other intermediate points of accommodation can be found in 'Where to Stay in Scotland' an Annual Spring publication of the Scottish Tourist Board, obtainable through main stationers. This lists both hotels and private houses, and it is as well to remember that during the tourist season (May to September) accommodation is best booked ahead. During the school holiday period (July-August) tourist traffic on the main roads is very great and pressure on bed space is accordingly intense. Accommodation lists are also available from local County Council offices. Indiscriminate roadside camping is generally discouraged but many camp sites are available by arrangement on the croft land, and several larger public camp sites exist alongside the main roads. Visitors unfamiliar with the area should ask their motoring organization for lists, or refer to one or other of the Camping or Caravan Site guides which become available at booksellers throughout the country in the Spring of each year.

Away from the main roads, of course, conditions change and in many parts of the area it is still unusual to meet another climbing group. The more remote parts of the ground offer great scope for the camper-climber and it is by far the best way to explore the hills. Good equipment is needed, however, because of the rain and wind combination which is common in the narrow western valleys. Properly, of course, permission to camp should be asked at all times, but in practice the wilder areas have no restriction except in certain places mentioned in the detailed accounts which follow, or during the stalking season. Continuation of this freedom depends to a large degree on the campers themselves. Please leave no litter and bury all tins deeply. Foxes or badgers will have them up if you do not, and cause serious injury to deer, sheep and hill cattle.

For those without cars, however, the question of how to get into the camping areas is of more importance. There is a bus route along the Great Glen, with a fairly frequent service. There is of course a rail service to Mallaig and a bus service along Locheilside. There are services from the Great Glen to Achnacarry, Kinloch Hourn, Shiel Bridge (for Kyle and Arnisdale) and Tomich (Strath Glass), also Inverness to Tomich and to Achnasheen. If the rail service Dingwall to Kyle is withdrawn it will be replaced by a bus. Apart from those in the Great Glen and others from Inverness, the services are not necessarily daily and have varied from year to year, so beware. A timetable, 'Getting Around the Highlands', is prepared by the Highlands and Islands Development Board, Bridge House, Bank Street, Inverness [Tel. 0463-34171] and you want sections 2 and 3. At the time of writing these cost 6p each.

Access to land
Most of the hill country in the Western Highlands lies on privately owned estates which derive a greater or lesser proportion of their revenue from stalking and fishing. A few important areas such as Glen Affric are leased or owned by the Forestry Commission, while the Five Sisters of Kintail and Ben Attow belong to the National Trust for Scotland.

The *Scottish Geographical Magazine*, Vol. LXXV, 1968, has published an estate map and descriptive text from which the areas and names of the estates can be derived. Unfortunately, for fiscal and other reasons, no contact addresses could be given.

Climbers wishing to have formal contact with estates say to arrange access in the stalking season or for a youth club camp are therefore posed with something of a problem. In practice, practically all of the estates within which the most popular mountains lie can be contacted, eventually, by writing to 'The Proprietor or Head Keeper'. The estate name can be got from the S.G.M. and the address should be the name of the main glen on which the estate abuts. In most cases the postal village is the nearest one in the Great Glen for those east of the watershed or the nearest community on the west side. The Post Office has a happy knack of sorting things out in the Highlands.

For the Forestry Commission land the Forestry Commission (Scotland) 25 Drumsheugh Gardens, Edinburgh 3, can no doubt forward queries to their local officers. The National Trust for Scotland resides at 5 Charlotte Square, Edinburgh 2.

In some cases more detailed information about contact addresses has been given in the sectional descriptions.

History
The District is full of historical associations of the 1745 Jacobite rising, echoes of which can still be faintly heard from place to place and which is the foundation of many legends which, probably, are no stranger than the truth. Other shadowy figures stride the Glens. The 15th Century Lords of the Isles on the western seaboard; James I of Scotland at Invergarry; Colkitto MacDonald, the left-handed warrior who, with his Irish fighting men *en route* to assist Montrose in support of Charles I, burnt one or two of the old castles and General Monk of the Commonwealth forces who rectified matters by building forts; General Wade, road-builder (and so indirect pacifier of the Clans) with his shares in the Strontian Lead Mines; Banquo (if he existed) at Tor Castle and of course the unknown men who built the Brochs of Glenelg and the vitrified forts of Kinlochteacuis and elsewhere. These folk, with their latter-day colleagues, the Commandos, will be referred to in the appropriate sectional chapters.

Geology
If one stands on any high peak in the Western Highlands (or for that

matter in any part of the Highlands of Scotland) the surrounding summits appear to merge in the distance to form a flat horizon. It is easy to appreciate from such a view that the country is not made up of individual mountains thrown up by earth movements such as folding or faulting, but are rather the remnants of a vast, more or less plateau-like upland surface. What appears from below to be separate hills are really the serrated ridges left between the valleys of rivers which are slowly eating into this plateau. (Photo 3.)

The origins of this Highland Plateau go far back in geological time, but it was essentially formed about 50 million years ago when land started to emerge from the sea over what is now Scotland. As it rose, it formed a broad arch whose axis ran N-S forming a watershed off which rivers flowed in relatively straight courses which trended west or east. These rivers and the waves of the surrounding seas wore down the land mass almost as quickly as it emerged, stripping from it layers of soft sedimentary rock which had been laid down over several geological epochs to lay bare a core of hard, crystalline strata forming the basement to the sedimentary accumulation. This basement proved a rather more formidable adversary to the agents of erosion. Although it, too, was planated to an almost plateau-like surface, it rose more quickly than the seas and rivers could wear it down and now forms the 'High Land' area. Although the present watershed does not necessarily coincide precisely with the original one, the east-and-west flowing rivers have inherited their course from the original drainage pattern and are still doing their best to wear this land away, aided now by a ramifying system of tributaries. The Highland Plateau thus has been dissected into the ridge-mountain systems which we now see. Fortunately for 'Munro baggers' much of the old plateau surface is at or about 3000 ft. above sea level!

Naturally, weak strata are eroded preferentially and one especially weak line was that of the Great Glen of Scotland which follows the line of a great geological fault. This has shattered the rock over a width of half a mile or more, isolating the Western and Northern Highlands (of the S.M.C. classification) from the adjacent Grampian block to the south. There are good geological reasons for believing that along the line of the Great Glen Fault, strata were displaced *laterally* not vertically, this lateral displacement being of the order of 65 miles. In other words, what is now the Glen Tarbert area formerly lay opposite Foyers. Some argue for a displacement in the opposite direction.

The hard core of crystalline rocks which make up the Highlands of Scotland belong mainly to the class which the geologist calls metamorphic. That is, they have been metamorphosed (had their form changed) from their original state. In the Western Highlands the strata were originally sandstones or shales (or in places a mixture of alternate laminae of the two types) laid down as sediments in a shallow sea around 900 million years ago. About 500 million years ago, however, these rocks were caught up in a zone of profound crustal movement between two continental masses and subjected to immense pressures, accompanied, over most of the area, by a great increase of crustal temperature. As a result their chemical constituents became re-arranged to form new minerals which crystallized in interlocking mosaics to render the rocks very tough and resistant. Sandstones became 'quartz-feldspar-granulites' usually called 'psammitic granulites' and shales became 'mica-schists' or 'pelitic schists'. The laminated rocks became 'striped schists'.

As part of the intense re-crystallization of the rocks of the area, innumerable tiny clots, threads and lenses of coarse granite were formed which grew in an intimate mixture with the mica-schists and striped schists to form one of the many varieties of the parallel-banded rock known as 'gneiss'. Excess of this coarse granite crystallized out in thick veins criss-crossing the metamorphic strata in all directions. These coarse granites are known as 'pegmatites' and are common in the mica-schist areas. The veins are mainly white or sometimes pale pink and in the white varieties the mineral mica often shows up as silvery plates several inches across.

Deep down below the Western Highlands the metamorphism was so intense that the earth's crust was partially fused to form molten rock which rose upwards to consolidate on cooling within the overlying schists and gneisses as the crystalline igneous rock, granite (much finer in grain than the pegmatite variety). Much more rarely, gabbro rose from even greater depths.

The distribution of these rocks in the Western Highlands is shown in the accompanying geological map. The complex outcrop pattern of the metamorphic rocks is largely as a result of folding of the strata during the metamorphic period. It can be inferred from the map that the folds of this 'Caledonian' episode are in places of immense size, but folds on all scales down to minute puckers can be found in all rock exposures. They are especially obvious in the mica-schist or striped schist areas.

SKETCH MAP OF THE GEOLOGY OF THE WESTERN HIGHLANDS

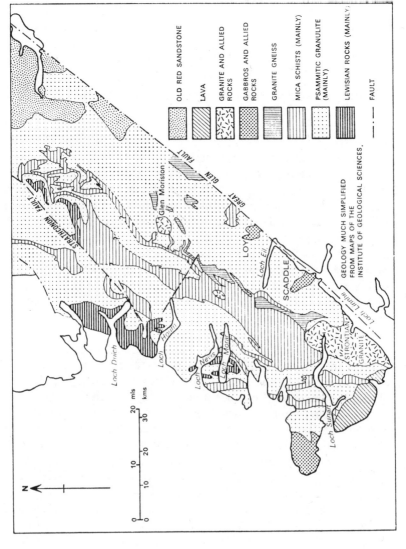

OLD RED SANDSTONE

LAVA

GRANITE AND ALLIED ROCKS

GABBROS AND ALLIED ROCKS

GRANITE GNEISS

MICA SCHISTS (MAINLY)

PSAMMITIC GRANULITE (MAINLY)

LEWISIAN ROCKS (MAINLY)

FAULT

GEOLOGY MUCH SIMPLIFIED FROM MAPS OF THE INSTITUTE OF GEOLOGICAL SCIENCES.

N

20 mls
kms
0   10   20   30

STRATHCONON FAULT

GLEN FAULT

GREAT GLEN FAULT

Glen Moriston

LOY

SCADDLE

STRONTIAN GRANITE

Loch Limnhe

Loch Eil

Loch Duich

Loch Hourn

Loch Nevis

Loch Morar

Loch Sunart

Granulites usually crop out as pale, flaggy-banded yet smoothly-weathering, crags or slabs. Mica-schists make up much more knobbly ground, especially where they are mixed with granite to form gneisses. They are laminated rocks, quite readily split along innumerable parallel parting planes to give lustrous, mica-coated silvery surfaces, although the rock in bulk is dark grey. Granites are massive and smooth weathering, usually pale grey or pale pink in colour, while gabbros of the Caledonian period are very dark in colour although in detail are mottled black and white.

In the extreme tip of the peninsula of Ardnamurchan, however, gabbros and allied rocks of a different age are found. These form part of a great volcanic centre, one of several which were active along the western seaboard and islands of Scotland about 60 million years ago, during the Tertiary period (see S.M.C. District Guide, *The Island of Skye*). What is seen in Ardnamurchan is not the old volcano proper, but rather its deep roots, represented by the solidified molten rock which first fed the outpouring lavas and, latterly, rose up to invade the collapsed base of the volcano itself. The structure is incredibly complex in detail, but in general is formed of a series of concentric rings.

Gabbro and the allied rock type, dolerite, of Tertiary age commonly weather smooth and massive, but are rough in detail and seamed with cracks which give good holds to the climber. Although the rock is black in colour when fresh, it commonly weathers in shades of rusty brown. Thin parallel sided vertical 'dykes' of dolerite extend well beyond the Tertiary centres and are sparsely distributed in the Western Highlands. In the Morar area, however, they are common, but are not always easy to distinguish from a suite of similar dyke rocks of much earlier (Permian) age which are also of widespread occurrence, especially in the Loch Eil and Morvern areas.

Near Loch Aline are found sparse remnants of the sediments which covered the Highland metamorphic rocks. These are sandstones and shales, mainly of Jurassic age, which have been preserved west of Loch Arienas under a capping of Tertiary lavas which flowed from either the Mull or Ardnamurchan volcanic centres. The white sandstone of Lochaline is mined and crushed to make a glass sand.

Like all of the Highland area of Scotland the Western Highlands show spectacular evidence of the Glacial Period which commenced perhaps one million, and ended about ten thousand, years ago. At its maximum, a great ice-cap more or less covered the area but what is now most evident are the effects of the last stages of glaciation – the 'valley glacier' period. At that time glaciers, flowing east and west from a median line somewhat east of the present watershed debouched through the main river valleys to the sea on the west and the Great Glen on the east. To start with these valleys probably had the V-shaped cross-section of river erosion, but this was sculptured to a broad U-shape by the action of the glaciers. Near the glacier divide evidence of ice-moulding is readily seen in detail in the bare, glacially-smoothed slabs and small hummocks – the roches moutonnées – which can be found in the valley sides and floors. These latter have a smooth slope facing the glacier impact side and a steep small crag on the pluck, or downstream, side relative to the glacier flow. At higher levels, small glaciers lingered long in the hollows of the hills, eating back into the rock with freeze-thaw action to excavate the cup-shaped corries at the heads of the main and tributary valleys. As they encroached on the ridge tops from either side, so they narrowed them and in places cut through them so that peaks are commonly isolated by depressions with narrow ridge-crests.

It is in the western sea-lochs, however, that the glacier action is most spectacular. Along these long, narrow, fiord-like trenches the upper reaches are often steep and narrow, while the glacier, compressed in these trenches, cut deeply downwards as well as sideways. Loch Morar, for instance, has a depth of about 1080 ft. about one third of the way inland from its seaward end. As the erosive power of the ice declined, either because of widening of the original valley or because the glacier floated on reaching the sea, the glacial overdeepening commonly diminished rapidly towards the end of the fiords, which therefore often have a rock lip near their exits, or at least partway along their length.

Glacial moraines are almost absent from the western part of the area, but the eastern valleys become clothed in these deposits left by the ice more and more from west to east. In the Great Glen thick sand and gravel deposits washed out from the glacier snouts are seen at the confluence of the side glens with the main valley, where they form relatively fertile flats.

As far as climbing is concerned it must be admitted that the rocks are not well suited to the harder arts of the sport. The area is divided into four main districts, geologically. Referring to the map, the ground east of the mica-schist belt is made up of granulite which tends to occur in flat-lying beds of very even composition so that there are few places where differential erosion can give rise to craggy ground. West of the mica-schist belt the granulites and interbedded mica-schists lie steeply in complex folds and often form cliffs where the rocks, however, tend to be slabby, with vegetatious cracks. Locally as in Kintail some satisfactory climbs are to be found. The big cliffs of Ladhar Bheinn, however, do not seem adapted for good rock-climbing. The main mica-schist belt makes up very rugged ground indeed but, as the rocks are intensely folded on all scales the crags have few continuous lines on them for the climber to follow, while in detail, the rock is rather friable and vegetatious. Where shot through by granite to form gneiss, however, the mica-schist and granulite can supply some fine climbing rock, as at Garbh Bheinn of Ardgour and the hills around Loch Shiel and Glen Dessary. Unfortunately only in the first area are the crags sufficiently continuous to give good sport.

Of the igneous rocks, the Tertiary complex of Ardnamurchan has good, though short, climbs on gabbro and allied rocks. The granites and earlier gabbros of the area, though potentially good, lack crags. Short climbs on these rocks are mentioned in the appropriate regional sections.

Wild Life

In twenty years' work in the hills of the Western Highlands the author has had the opportunity of seeing a fair spectrum of the animal and bird population which lives in the area. Any others which he or his colleagues have not seen are probably unlikely to be found by the casual visitor and will be sought after only by the specialist naturalist who will probably have no need of help from this book to locate their habitat!

Red deer, of course, are the most common of the larger mammals and are to be found in great numbers throughout the area. Indeed, they can be a pest to the local crofters during the spring when they invade the arable land in search of food. Any day on the hill one is liable to meet with a small herd which makes off at speed on sensing the approach of humans. On a summer evening if one is camping in the remote glens one often suddenly becomes aware that the valley has filled with small groups drifted down from the tops in uncanny silence to feed on the grass by the river. Commonly dozens of beasts can be counted at one time and it is difficult to realize that they have all come from the same hills where, during the day, only a few have been seen.

Early in the season – in the late spring and early summer – the writer has not found that red deer are particularly timid. The animals are intent on feeding on the new growth and will often graze up to within a few yards of a person sitting quietly making notes or eating lunch. On one summer evening in Glen Dessarry the writer was adopted by a deer-calf strayed from a passing group of hinds and this, despite efforts to shoo it away, followed him for half-a-mile until it was retrieved by an agitated parent. Later on, in July and August, the beasts become more readily disturbed, while during the rut, in September and October, it is sometimes the human who is agitated on the fearless approach of a large stag intent on defending his harem. The largest number of red deer which the author has seen in the area was at Easter in Glen Quoich where he and an S.M.C. party counted over six hundred beasts in three miles of glen at a time when the hills were deep in snow.

Roe deer are common in the wooded areas, especially around the Great Glen and are frequently found in Forestry Commission plantings where their presence is unwelcome because of damage they are reputed to do to young trees. When startled, they go bounding off with a repeated, sharp, dog-like bark. Local opinion credits them with being ferocious if unduly alarmed.

Foxes are by no means rare in the area and are actively kept down by the keepers and even, at the time of writing, by a pack of foot-followed hounds. As they are wary animals they are most often seen at a distance, especially from above. In winter pad-marks on the snow along ridge crests give their presence away. Badgers are fairly common. Although normally nocturnal they have been seen in daylight three times by the writer. Their sets can usually be identified by scars of freshly turned earth and rejected bedding. Unfortunately local crofters credit them with raiding habits second only to the fox and harry them accordingly. They are usually found in the wooded areas but also live in surprising barren glens remote from trees or croft-land.

Otters can be found in the major rivers or inland lochs and can sometimes be met with quite far from water, as on one occasion near Garrygualach in Glen Garry when the author met one at least a mile from the nearest loch.

Wildcat are rare but have been seen on Loch Arkaig side and in Glen Garry and a pine marten was seen by one of the writer's colleagues in Glen Moriston.

Squirrels, stoats and the usual small animals can be found in the appropriate places. Rats seem to continue habitation of deserted bothies for decades after the human occupants have gone and even food hung from rafters and encased in several layers of groundsheet is not safe from their attack!

Ardgour ('Goat Heights') is traditionally the home of wild goats and the author can vouch for the presence of a large and somewhat aggressive herd on the hills to the south east of Loch Shiel. Probably many of these are domestic goats gone feral. They are also found around the head of Loch Morar.

While working on the hills above Loch Ness the writer and two colleagues recorded the presence of an 'unidentified swimming object' near Castle Urquhart. While this was probably the Monster, it could just possibly have been a seal. These animals are known to enter the north end of the Loch in pursuit of salmon up the River Ness, but if this was one, it was far from home. Undoubted seals are common along the western coasts and in the sea-lochs and canoe-borne climbers in Loch Nevis and Loch Hourn can study them at close quarters at various 'seal islands'. The skerries off Arisaig are full of them and a canoeist should remember that his craft may look rather like an alien seal to a local beast. It is as well to be rather wary in one's approach.

If a climber in the Western Highlands thinks he has seen an eagle the chances are probably about a hundred to one that it is a buzzard! Nonetheless eagles are by no means uncommon and have been seen by the author at one time or another from Ardgour to Glen Affric, especially over the rugged western hills, but from place to place in the eastern glens as well. At a distance there is no easy way to distinguish the larger and smaller birds although to an experienced eye the soaring character of the eagle's flight is almost certainly recognizeable from that of the buzzard. The writer maintains against all opposition that buzzards always look more 'hump-backed' in flight than an eagle, whose head appears to stick out more ahead of the wings. At close quarters there is no doubt when the size of the bird can be made out. Herons can be found along the shores of all the sea lochs and their ragged nests can be seen in woods quite far inland. Of the other large birds Black-throated Diver are relatively common on the inland lochs while the usual selection of ducks can be met with in appropriate places. Grouse are not plentiful except in the lower hills to the east. Blackcock are sufficiently abundant for the author and his colleagues to have twice inadvertently camped in the middle of a 'lek' ground, both times in the Loch Arkaig area and they have been treated to a magnificent courtship display from the impromptu 'hides' provided by their tents. Unfortunately the performance on both occasions started at dawn when sleepy geologists are hardly at their most appreciative of the bubbling, pops and gobbles which seem to be a necessary accompaniment to the interminable proceedings.

The hill country has the usual assemblage of smaller birds including ptarmigan, curlew, ring ousel, golden plover, greenshank and dipper. Sandpiper are daily companions on any walk up a river bank in summer, their fluttering flight and call being distinctive. Wagtails, too, are very common and oyster-catchers, with their bold black, white and orange colours are easily seen along any of the gravelly banks of major streams. Camping in the glens near the river marshes on a summer evening the flute-notes of snipe 'drumming' is a common, and rather eerie, sound, while the bird's incessant 'wee-chip, wee-chip, wee-chip' call makes a constant background noise.

The climber, unless he is an ornithologist, will tend to ignore the innumerable, less-remarkable types but perhaps he will find it difficult, in the early summer, to avoid seeing the white flash on the rump of a wheatear which arrives in large numbers, and, if he is sitting anywhere near a tourist attraction, the importuning chaffinch will no doubt persuade him to share his lunch. They can often be hand-fed.

In the woods, of course, there is a vast selection of 'tweety' birds which will keep the specialist happy during his holiday, but these are best left to ornithological books to describe. Perhaps it is as well for climbing bird-watchers that there are not many large woods in the more mountainous areas!

The Hydro-Electric Development

Climbers and walkers in the Western Highlands cannot avoid being impressed by the massive dams and great lochs of the electric power development of the area. Nearly every major valley has been exploited by the North of Scotland Hydro-Electric Board in projects which, starting in the area soon after the last War, continued in construction until about 1965.

The Garry-Moriston Project, with a total output potential of 113 megawatts involves major dams at the east end of Loch Quoich (the largest rock-fill dam in Britain) and Loch Garry, the power being generated at Quoich and Invergarry Stations. Loch Quoich, ponded back by the main dam, flooded westwards over an area of rather desolate marshland towards the narrow defile of the Carnoch River. As loch level was raised above the watershed there, two cut-off dams were constructed near Lochan nam Breac. In Glen Loyne a major dam impounded a reservoir which floods back into Glen Quoich over the former Tomdoun–Cluanie road and 'tops up' the main reservoir of Loch Cluanie in Glenmoriston. The dam there is of especial interest in that it was designed to make use, in times of cement shortage, of the special properties of pulverized fuel ash which was used to 'bulk out' the concrete. The power station for this section is at Ceannacroc but the water is again used further down Glen Moriston at Dundreggan Dam. There the water, augmented by the outflow from a subsidiary scheme on the hills to the north, falls in a vertical tunnel below the dam to Glenmoriston underground power station. The spent water then has a long run in a tailrace tunnel to Invermoriston where it enters Loch Ness.

The tributaries of the Beauly River provide individual schemes in their own right. In Glen Cannich, the huge Mullardoch Dam impounds an immense reservoir, flooding back over the former rather bleak upper reaches of the Glen almost to Glen Elchaig. The water from this reservoir flows by tunnel to Glen Affric where it is used to top-up the reservoir in Glen Affric impounded by the Benevean Dam. As a result the loch in this lovely Glen is rarely drawn down to an unsightly degree. Power from the two valleys is generated at the Fasnakyle Generating Station near Cannich (66 megawatts).

Glen Strathfarrar is used in a stage-by-stage scheme based on the elegant double-curvature arch dam (the first in Britain) which impounds an enlarged Loch Monar. The water from this loch is used several times by diversion tunnels on its way to join the River Glass at Struie (output 62 megawatts).

These three tributary valleys, Affric Cannich and Strathfarrar supply water to the River Glass which, becoming the Beauly River, is in turn utilized in a stage-by-stage scheme at the Aigas and Kilmorack Dams (each 20 megawatts).

A similar complex further north utilizes the catchment from the Dirrie Mor area, the Loch Fannich area, the Loch Luichart area and Strath Orrin in a complex of reservoirs, tunnels and power stations of which only these of Glen Orrin (18 megawatts) and Loch Luichart (24 megawatts) fall within the present Guide Book area.

Smaller schemes utilize the great volume of Loch Morar (the first operational post-War scheme – 750 kw.) and the high head available from the ground between Ardelve and Strome Ferry (The Kyle of Loch Alsh Scheme).

While these schemes have their critics on the grounds of interference with natural features and the inevitable violation of the wilderness character of much of the country, on the whole they have been handled with respect to the amenity of the area. The scars of former years have mellowed and it is doubtful if climbers of today who read this book will find much to regret about the lost land. After all, 'Strength of the Glens' (the N.S.H.E.B. slogan) is something no-one can despise and many can be proud of.

On one point only the present author feels aggrieved. Along the side of the enlarged Quoich and Mullardoch Reservoirs no paths now exist. The going there is execrable! No doubt, however, this makes some contribution to accentuating the wilderness character that remains!

BIBLIOGRAPHY

The volumes of the Scottish Mountaineering Club Journal of course form the main source of detailed information concerning the hills of the Western Highlands District and it is hardly necessary to detail these articles, as adequate volume indexes are available for the researcher. The S.M.C. *Climber's Guide to Glencoe and Ardgour Vol. 2 – Glencoe, Beinn Trilleachan and Garbh Bheinn* is the authoritative work on the rock climbs on the latter mountain. No other rock climbing guide to the hills is as yet available and the Appendix to this volume is an interim measure to meet this lack. A private publication by R. Frere *Rock Climbs* was printed in 1938 and dealt in part with short climbs on the hills on the north side of Loch Ness from Drumnadrochit to Inverness. Unfortunately this has not been available to the author since he revised the last edition of this Guide.

More general publications of interest are as follows –

REGIONAL
Romantic Lochaber, Donald B. MacCulloch. Moray Press, Edinburgh. This is the authoritative work on that part of Lochaber lying within the Western Highlands District, i.e. Glen Garry south to Loch Eil. It is a mine of information but is best appreciated by the initiated.
Moidart and Morar, Wendy Wood. Moray Press, Edinburgh, 1950.
The Drove Roads of Scotland, A. R. B. Haldane. University Press,

Edinburgh, 1966. Amongst its complete coverage of the subject this refers to the routes from Skye across the Western Highlands.

New Ways Through the Glens, A. R. B. Haldane. Thos. Nelson and Sons, Edinburgh, 1962. This deals with the first construction of the post-military highways.

The West Highland Railway, John Thomas. Pan Books, 1970. Tales of the Fort William to Mallaig extension and of the ill-starred Invergarry and Fort Augustus branch line.

HISTORY

The history of the area is largely bound up with the '45 Rising:

The Lyon in Mourning, Bishop Forbes (3 vols.) Scot. Hist. Soc. 1895, is the authoritative work on the subject but most people will be adequately served by:

The Prince in the Heather, Eric Linklater. Hodder and Stoughton 1965.

Glenfinnan and the '45, National Trust for Scotland Handbook. Available from the Trust (see pp. 16 and 51).

Also of historical interest are:-

A Tour of the Hebrides with Dr. Johnson, James Boswell. Various publications of this classic. It has some interesting references to the Glen Moriston and Glen Shiel areas in 1773.

The (New) Statistical Account of the parishes of Scotland by Ministers of the Church, 1845 ca. This contains some interesting, if sometimes questionable stories about the past history of the parishes. It also contains fascinating accounts of the condition of the area at the time the chapters were written.

NATURAL HISTORY

No one book deals with the Western Highlands either specifically or by specific subject.

Natural History in the Highlands and Islands, Frank Fraser Darling and J. Morton Boyd. Fontana New Naturalist (paperback) 1969, is an authoritative general work applicable to the Western Highlands.

British Regional Geology Scotland: The Northern Highlands; and *Scotland The Tertiary Volcanic Areas*. Handbooks of the Geological Survey H.M.S.O. These are two general accounts including, respectively, the Western Highlands (excluding the volcanic areas) and Ardnamurchan. They are relatively simple accounts, best appreciated by those with at least a little geological knowledge. They are revised at intervals, as, though the rocks do not change, the state of the science does.

The writer is seldom without two useful volumes in his car. These are, *A Field Guide to the Birds of Britain and Europe* (Collins) and *The Pocket Guide to the Wild Flowers* (also Collins). These suit his rather rudimentary knowledge of these subjects. Of course most folk will have their own pet books out of the many available.

Mountain Rescue

The availability of mountain rescue equipment and the provision of local mountain rescue teams is apt to vary from time to time. It is best in all cases where help is required to contact the local Police who have mountain rescue arrangements specially prepared and can summon local or district rescue teams at need. At the moment the arrangements for the Western Highlands are on a county basis centred on Dingwall and Fort William but this situation is likely to change if proposed re-arrangement of local administrative areas takes place. At any rate an emergency telephone call to "Police" will set the machinery in operation.

The Western Highlands has many very remote areas within it and there have been several accidents in recent years to solo hill walkers whose whereabouts and return-schedules were imperfectly known. The Inverness-shire Police are distributing forms to various places of public resort which you would do well to complete giving your plans for mountain journeys. Camper-climbers have however a special problem and a special responsibility to ensure that someone knows of their whereabouts. Forms can be had from the Police at Fort William.

1

Morvern

Creach Bheinn, 2800 ft. (872577)*
Maol Odhar, 2578 ft. (883577)
Beinn Mheadhoin, 2423 ft. (799515)
Beinn Iadain, 1873 ft. (692562)
Sithean na Raplaich, 1806 ft. (636517)

Maps: One-inch Ordnance Survey, 7th Series, Sheets 45, 46. Half-inch Bartholomew
    latest edition, Sheet 47.

* Figures in brackets are National Grid References.

It is a pity that on any logical description of the mountains of the
Western Highlands the account must either start or finish with areas
which, to the writer, are the least attractive. Not that they are by an
means scenically deficient, but from the mountaineer's point of view
they are overshadowed by the magnificent hills of the central part of
the area. The author of the original District Guide stated that the
hills of Morvern are more attractive to look from than to look at, and
the present writer sees no reason to disagree.

The higher hills lie to the west of the Strontian–Lochaline road
and are made up either of granite or metamorphic rocks with many
veins of granite. They are smooth-contoured with some well-formed
corries. The central part of the peninsula is made up of various
schists (map, page 19) but west of Lochs Aline, Arienas and Teacuis
the hills are tabular in form, being carved out of horizontal flows of
basalt lavas of Tertiary age, like much of the adjacent northern part of
Mull and Northern Skye. They present quite a respectable escarpment to the east, with large, open corries. Outlying patches of lava
cap some of the hills to the east of the loch line, notably forming
Beinn Iadain (1873 ft.). The lava-featuring is also seen east of Loch
Aline as at An Dunan, where the flat-lying layers crop out in a circle
and probably account both for its colloquial name of Table of Lorne
and its original Gaelic likening to a Dun or fort.

The main road from Strontian to Lochaline is now well-graded and surfaced, being a main access to the Isle of Mull car ferry. The loop road from Inversanda to the Lochaline road is narrow, but has interesting coastal views. Other roads are the spur to Kinlochteacuis and the continuation of the main road from Loch Aline to Drimnin. The latter road can be continued by a rough track round the western point of the peninsula to Dorlinn, but there is no public carriageway. Around Loch Aline and the Kinlochteacuis area the scenery is pleasant rather than spectacular, with good views of the Sound of Mull from the main road continuation. Loch Teacuis is a pretty and secluded spot. Much new forestry work has been and is still being, undertaken in the area.

Ardtornish Castle on the shores of the Sound of Mull south of Loch Aline was a stronghold of the Lords of the Isles in the fifteenth century. Kinlochaline Castle was burnt in 1664 by Colkitto MacDonald and his Irish soldiery during his support of the Montrose uprising (see also Mingarry Castle p. 43). Nothing seems to be known about Glendsanda Castle on the remote shores of Loch Linnhe, but it was possibly a MacDougall building of relatively recent date.

There is a vitrified fort near Rahoy, Kinlochteacuis. This is one of many in the Western Highlands but is of special interest in that a model 'Gaelic Wall' was built there of the same material from which the fort was constructed. This was deliberately fired to test the various theories concerning the origin of the vitrification. The stones fused, but the argument between the proponents of deliberate or accidental (or hostile) combustion still remains.

Lochaline has deposits of a very pure glass sand, part of a group of strata which underly the lavas all the way along the escarpment. This is worked at the moment in a mine and exported by sea from the pier. Other beds of this sequence are highly fossilferous and it is worthwhile spending a few moments by the roadside a few hundred yards south-west of the Teacuis road turn off to collect specimens of *Gryphaea incurva*, an early variety of oyster, which over-developed its curves to such an extent that it died out because, paleontologists tell us, it could not open its mouth! These rather talon-like shells are found up the forestry side road and are colloquially called 'Devil's Toenails'.

Creach Bheinn, 2800 ft. – This mountain stands on the south side of Glen Tarbert and overlooks Loch Linnhe. It has two summits, the lower one, Maol Odhar (*c.* 2578 ft.), being ¾ mile E.N.E. from the higher one. To the north it throws out two fine ridges or shoulders

1. The industrial fringe. The paper pulp mill at Fort William and Glen Suileag
behind.

2. In the Great Glen. Cloud rises from the slopes of Meall na Teanga. Laggan Locks in foreground.

3. The accordant summits of the Highland plateau: the Grampians from Sgurr nan Coireachain, Glen Dessarry.

4. Red Deer Calf about two weeks old. Coire Ghiubhsachain, Loch Shiel

5. Maol Odhar (of Creach Bheinn).

6. Beinn Iadain, showing the tabular lava flows overlying schists.

Inst. Geol. Sciences

7. The Hills of Ardgour. Corran Ferry and Garbh Bheinn, whose Great Ridge shows up as a narrow triangle.

enclosing Coire nam Frithallt, the corrie to the north of Maol Odhar, not named on the one-inch map. The main summit of Creach Bheinn stands up rather imposingly at the head of Glen Galmadale. From Maol Odhar a long ridge runs southwards for 3½ miles, ending at Rubha na h-Airde Uinnsinn on the shore of Loch Linnhe. The southern part of this ridge is called Druim na Maodalaich, and its eastern slope, A'Mhaodalach, overhanging the narrow road along the shore of Loch Linnhe, is remarkably steep, consisting of great masses of reddish granite cut up by innumerable basalt dykes forming gullies and chimneys, unfortunately useless for climbing.

Possibly the simplest route to the top of Creach Bheinn is to take the Kingairloch road from Inversanda to Lochan Doire a' Bhraghaid, to a parking place at the top of the first hill, beside a lochan. The road should be followed for a short distance farther, and a line then struck up the valley to the west to the east top of Maol Odhar (c. 2207 ft.) and along a narrow ridge to the summit of Maol Odhar. A further walk of about twenty-five minutes takes one to the top of Creach Bheinn on which there is a big cairn. A local story is to the effect that this cairn was built as a watch-tower in the times of the Napoleonic wars! More probably it was built by the Ordnance Survey.

Beinn Mheadhoin, 2423 ft. is the prominent hill standing at the head of Kingairloch. There are several rather fine-looking corries on its N.E. face, but apparently they offer nothing worth climbing. Its east spur, Sgùrr a' Bhuic (1863 ft.), has a fine rocky summit and looks well from the N.E.

Sithean na Raplaich, 1860 ft. is the highest point of the hilly country lying to the north west of Loch Aline, from which it is five miles distant. With the exception of its N.E. escarpment of basaltic rock, the hill possesses no special feature of interest other than the magnificent view to be had from its summit in clear weather. It is now more or less surrounded by forest. Enquire at the Loch Aline forestry offices about access. This will depend on the state of the forestry roads, some of which go right up to the plateau.

Beinn Iadain, 1873 ft. The author has not climbed this mountain, the highest in the Lochaline area, but from the map it looks as though it should be approachable from Kinlochteacuis or from Acharn, on the main road near the outflow of Loch Arienas. There are some rather sinister-looking marshland symbols on the one-inch map at the head of the Arienas Burn. Under the summit rocks of Ben Iadain some sedimentary strata intervene between the flat lavas and the metamorphic rocks. Of these, the topmost layer is an attenuated band of barely recognizable Chalk, only 14 inches or so thick, a poor relation of the Cliffs of Dover!

Paths

The track from Drimnin to Dorlinn has been mentioned. A forestry road runs along the south side of Loch Sunart from Laudale House towards Glencripesdale. It has pleasant views towards Ardgour and Ardnamurchan.

Reference

The Experimental Production of the Phenomena distinctive of Vitrified Forts, V. Gordon Childe and W. Thorneycroft, Proc. Soc. Antiquaries of Scotland, Vol. 22, 1938.

2

Ardgour and Sunart

Garbh Bheinn, 2903 ft. (904622)
Sgor Mhic Eacharna, 2130 ft. (928630)
Beinn Bheag, 2387 ft. (905634)
Ben Resipol, 2775 ft. (765654)
Sgurr na h-Eanchainne, 2395 ft. (998659)
Meall Dearg Choire nam Muc, 2409 ft. (979655)
Sgurr Dhomhnuill, 2915 ft. (889679)
Sgurr Ghiubhsachain, 2784 ft. (875751)

Maps: One-inch Ordnance Survey, 7th Series, Sheets 45, 46 (mainly), 35. Half-inch Bartholomew latest edition, Sheet 50.

The area described in this section extends from the upper reaches of Loch Sunart and Glen Tarbert in the south to Loch Eil in the north. The eastern boundary is Loch Linnhe, and the west is Loch Shiel and the road from Acharacle to Salen. None of the hills in the district reaches the 3000 ft. level but eight of them are over 2500 ft., Sgurr Dhomhnuill being the highest at 2915 ft.

The district is extremely rugged and the mountains are much more impressive than one would think from their comparatively low heights. Garbh Bheinn of Ardgour is certainly one of the finest rock crags on the mainland of Scotland.

The predominant rocks of the district are of the metamorphic variety, but granite is found around Strontian and gabbro in the hills west of Corran Ferry. Gneissic varieties of schist provide unusually good climbing for the Western Highlands in Garbh Bheinn, but the granite weathers into relatively low ground.

The area is notable for its fine glens, of which Glen Iubhair, with good rock scenery in its upper reaches, is probably the most interesting to the climber. Glen Gour – the Glen of the Goats – Glen Scaddle, and Cona Glen all have their own attractions. They represent the beheaded parts of the original drainage of Scotland, cut off from their continuation on the west side of Loch Linnhe by the overdeepening along the Great Glen Fault. Glen Tarbert, likewise a fragment of ancient drainage, certainly ranks high amongst scenic glens available to the motorist. It has (or had once) an unusual feature at its watershed where the Allt a' Chothruim – the Burn of the Balance – sometimes flowed towards Loch Sunart and sometimes to Loch Linnhe, depending on the state of gravel accumulation on its delta. The name has passed into scientific usage as 'corrom', the geomorphologists' term for a delta watershed. The culvert for the new road has temporarily tamed the natural vagaries of the burn.

Most climbers will be attracted by Garbh Bheinn and Sgurr Domhnuill and few will visit the other hills of the area although these are by no means unworthy of attention. A new, fast road from Corran Ferry (tolls on the ferry – for cost and times see motoring association handbooks) provides easy access to Glen Tarbert and Strontian. The alternative and interminable route *via* Loch Eil is narrow and suffers from tourist thrombosis in the summer.

Strontian itself is a pleasant place for car-ferrying non-climbing wives to spend the day and, indeed, has its own interest for out-of-doors folk. It has been moderately developed to encourage visitors to stay there and now offers enhanced accommodation and refreshment facilities. Handouts are available detailing excursions of natural interest and day fishing permits can be had.

There are old lead workings which are scattered over the nearby hills. These date from 1722 (General Wade was an early shareholder) and only ceased production in 1904. The old mine dumps contain a wide variety of interesting minerals for the 'rock-hound' or gemstone collector and, although none are precious, many are attractive. Probably the most interesting are the dull grey crystals of galena (lead sulphide) which when broken have a fine silvery metallic lustre. Strontianite, from which the mineral strontium was first obtained, is a rare find nowadays and is another instance of the area's contribution to scientific nomenclature.

In the valley of the Strontian River, an attractive walk along the track takes one to a Nature Conservancy area for the study of forest regeneration. Although it is fenced off there is still plenty of comparable ground around for examination.

Other features of general interest in the Ardgour area are the huge peat moss of Claish, near Acharacle, with its intriguing growth-patterns, and there are some fairish stands of old Caledonian pines south of Callop near Glenfinnan, although the latter trees are now being surrounded by new plantings.

The Ardgour goats, mentioned in the introduction, can be found in several places around the glen heads, especially near Loch Shiel.

Access to the hills has its problems. Along Loch Eil side new plantings obliterate several of the paths shown on the one-inch map, while certain of the estate proprietors show a preference for prior consultation before parties go on the hills. Especially those visiting Garbh Bheinn by way of Glen Iubhair have in the past been asked to make their presence known at Inversanda. Permission to camp should also be sought there. The writer has no knowledge of parties being refused access to any hill in recent years, except of course during the stalking season or during periods of sheep-gathering.

Garbh Bheinn, 2903 ft. This very fine mountain stands on the north side of Glen Tarbert, about 2½ miles west from Inversanda. It throws out two well-defined ridges, or shoulders, to the S.E. and S.W., which enclose the steep Coire a' Chothruim out of which flow the headwaters of the Carnoch River. The S.E. ridge is called Sron a' Gharbh Choire Bhig, and is named after the extremely slabby corrie, the Garbh Choire Beag, which is so conspicuous a feature of the S.W. slope of Glen Iubhair. The S.W. ridge leads down to Meall a' Chuilinn (2228 ft.), overlooking Glen Tarbert. Garbh Bheinn has two summits: the highest point, which is on the edge of the great eastern precipice, and the west top, which is 89 ft. lower, and stands a quarter of a mile W.N.W. of the other. To the north the peak of Garbh Bheinn drops down gradually, and then very steeply, to the Bealach Feith'n Amean, in which lies the little Lochan Coire an Iubhair (1753 ft.).

The main feature of Garbh Bheinn is its very precipitous eastern face, which towers above the little Garbh Choire Mor at the head of Glen Iubhair. The Great Ridge, which is about 1000 ft. in height, leads up to the actual summit, while the right-hand wall of the corrie is the Pinnacle Ridge, spectacular from below but disappointing at close quarters. The Great Gully – one of the last major gullies to be climbed in Scotland – bounds the Great Ridge on the right. The mountain is of contorted grey quartzo-feldspathic gneiss of the Moine Assemblage which offers splendid holds to the climber. The climbs on Garbh Bheinn and adjacent cliffs are described in the S.M.C. *Rock-Climbers' Guide to Glencoe and Ardgour*, Vol. II, 'Glencoe Beinn Trilleachan and Garbh Bheinn.'

The simplest routes up the mountain are by way of one or other of the S.E. and S.W. ridges, while the shortest way would be up the south corrie (Coire a' Chothruim) from the Strontian road, from which the summit is only 1¼ miles distant. The route up this corrie is, however, very steep and shut in, and it is not nearly so attractive as the ridge walk up the Sron a' Gharbh Choire Bhig. This ridge is well broken up with rocky outcrops, and it has good views.

In good weather the aesthetic approach to the mountain is by Glen Iubhair. This way however is rather boggy in wet weather and is dreary in mist, when the way to Garbh Bheinn summit is not easy to hit off. In fine weather the glen has some fine rocky scenery. First is the very steep and slabby Garbh Choire Beag on the west side of the glen. This has provided some rock climbs. The rocky Garbh Choire Mor, over which the grand peak of the mountain rises impressively, soon afterwards comes into view. The corrie can be entered by the burn which issues from it and a way easily made to the summit of Garbh Bheinn by way of the col between that mountain and Sron a' Garbh Choire Bhig. If Glen Iubhair is followed, however, it rises rapidly to the narrow Bealach Feith'n Amean, passing below the North-East Buttress and North Face of Garbh Bheinn. The North-East Buttress is very slabby and is divided horizontally by three rakes into four tiers. The third tier is the Leac Mhor (The Great Slab) and is reputed to be the greatest sheet of slab in Scotland. At its highest and widest points it measures 500 ft. by 300 ft.

The round of the skyline of Glen Iubhair is worth doing as it gives excellent changing views of the rocky face of Garbh Bheinn. It is best to start with Druim an Iubhair, on the east side of the glen, as then Garbh Bheinn lies in front as the scene develops. The Druim leads easily to Sgor Mhic Eacharna (2387 ft.) and from there one passes over the top of Beinn Bheag (2387 ft.) and point 2272 ft. on the map, until a steep descent can be made to Lochan Coire an Iubhair. The easiest route up the north slope of Garbh Bheinn is then by a talus slope to the right of the bealach leading to a narrow scree-shoot, which gives access to the little north-west corrie of the mountain at about 2400 ft. (If taken in reverse this bit can be tricky on the descent, especially in mist.) A walk up this corrie takes one on to the main ridge near the top of the Pinnacle Ridge, and so on to the summit cairn, which is perched almost on the edge of the Great Ridge. The route of descent is then down the south face of the peak, with grand views of the wonderful rock of the Great Ridge on one's left, to the high bealach (*c.* 2400 ft.) at the head of the Garbh Choire Mor, from which a short climb leads to the top of the Sron a' Gharbh Choire Bhig (2671 ft.) The ridge of the latter is then followed down to the road bridge over the river. The total round is about seven miles, with 4300 ft. of ascent.

Ben Resipol, 2775 ft. – This fine mountain is situated three miles north of Loch Sunart, about midway between Strontian and Salen. It is very prominent, being well isolated from its neighbours and is crowned by rocky masses which, from a distance, look as if they might afford some rock climbing, but on near acquaintance are disappointing. Its separate position, above two long lochs, and with low ground to the west, however, makes it a fine viewpoint and so its ascent on a good day is well worthwhile.

Probably the best approach is from Strontian by way of the old miners' track (shown on the map) from Scotstown to the former Corrantee (Coire an't–Suidhe) lead mines. (A car can be taken for a short distance.) From the watershed follow the track downwards to the first bend and then strike almost due west to hit the east end of the main ridge of Ben Resipol, which is followed to the summit.

The mountain can, of course, be climbed from several other directions, of which that from Resipol Farm on Loch Sunart is probably the most often used if one is coming from the west.

Sgurr na h-Eanchainne, 2395 ft. – This is the steep hill overlooking Ardgour, and its ascent is a favourite one for walking parties. The local name for it is Ben Keil, so named after the farm of that name at its base. There is no difficulty in the ascent provided that the steep rock bluffs guarding the lower part of the hill are avoided by turning their north end but a still easier way is to go up from Glen Gour, round Coire Dubh and pass over the actual top of the mountain, Meall Dearg Choire nam Muc (2409 ft.), which lies back about one mile W. by S. from the top of the Sgurr. The view from this is not so good. From the Coire Dubh on the east side of the Meall a very rapid stream descends in a succession of rapids and falls, which is called Ardgour's Towel. There are several fine falls in its lower portion which are well worth visiting after rain. The access is, however, through the precincts of Ardgour House and permission for the visit should be asked.

Sgurr Dhomhnuill, 2914 ft. – This is the highest mountain in the district. On account of its height and sharp appearance it is a conspicuous object when seen from a distance. It stands at the head of the

Strontian River glen, and is one of the numerous peaks surrounding the headwaters of the River Scaddle. The upper thousand feet of the mountain is very steep, especially the north face, which is rocky, but provides no real climbing. The southern slopes of the peak are not so steep and the ascent of them is quite simple. As the mountain stands a long way back from the coast its ascent by any route involves a fairly long day by any route.

The easiest and probably the most attractive way of climbing Sgurr Dhomhnuill is by the glen of the Strontian River. It has been possible to drive some distance up the glen but over the years the old bridges have become rather dangerous and the future situation will depend on their state of repair. The walk, however, is very pleasant, and leads first to the Feith Domhnuill lead mines, about six miles from Strontian. The summit can be gained easily from there by following up the stream on which the mines are situated.

Few people make the ascent from the east, up Glen Gour or Glen Scaddle, although these Glens are not without their attractions. Of the two, the writer would prefer Glen Gour, which has the more impressive scenery although involving a roundabout journey to reach the mountain from the head of the Glen. Loch nan Gobhar, at the mouth of the glen, was formerly raised by an ill-founded dam, whose ruins can be seen a few yards upstream from the old road bridge. The loch, and the marshy area around it, usually has a fair population of duck, swans and lesser water-birds.

Between Glen Gour and Corran Ferry the main road runs over a very flat area. This is made up of a great accumulation of gravel washed out from a glacier which, at the closing stage of the Glacial Period stood in Loch Linnhe. Immediately west of the Ferry, lochans in the flat probably represent the sites of large masses of ice which were engulfed in the gravel, subsequently melting away to give rise to these subsidence pits or 'Kettle holes'.

In the early part of the summer the wait at Corran Ferry can be less tedious if one is ornithologically minded. The bay north of the jetty on the Ardgour side is a good place for water-birds. Eider duck especially, are often seen here.

Sgurr Ghiubhsachain, 2784 ft. – Stretching northwards from Sgurr Dhomhnuill lies a very wild bit of country culminating in this fine mountain, which rises steeply from the south-east shore of Loch Shiel about four miles from the head of the loch. It and Beinn Odhar Mhor on the other side of the loch form the pair of the picturesque mountains which look so well in the view down Loch Shiel from Glenfinnan. Its ascent is worthwhile since, like Ben Resipol, it has a commanding position.

The ea iest way up Sgurr Ghiubhsachain is from Callop bridge about two miles east of Glenfinnan. A good Forestry Commission road (foot access only) leads from thence to Loch Shiel side and down to Guesachan cottage. From there the hill can be climbed either directly up its north ridge, or more pleasantly, by the burn which passes the cottage and the east ridge. A much more attractive way, however, is to climb Meall a' Bhainne, above Callop and follow the ridge over Meall Doire na Mnatha. The views all around from this ridge are very fine, especially those over the steep rocky buttresses on the west looking back towards Glenfinnan. There are some slabby scrambles to be had on these buttresses, on sound, rough rock and even the possibility of short genuine rock-climbs although these would be rather pointless, having neither length nor aesthetic attraction.

Paths

The construction of forestry access roads over some of the former paths of the area has made them less attractive to the walker than was once the case, while others, especially in the glen leading to Loch Eil, have been planted over, in part at least by private afforestation. Nevertheless there are some good scenic journeys to be had.

Although the new Forestry Commission road replacing the path on the south east side of Loch Shiel has destroyed the wild character of the walk, it is still worth doing. The section from Callop bridge to Guesachan cottage especially is very scenic. There is an alternative route from Callop to Polloch by way of the hill track to Glen Hurich. It is clearly marked on the one-inch and half-inch maps. From Polloch the old track past the Corrantee mines (see above) is an aesthetic alternative to the steep road from Loch Doilet to Scotstown near Strontian.

Through tracks to Glen Hurich run up both Cona Glen and Glen Scaddle, the writer finding the latter glen the more pleasant.

References

Undiscovered Scotland, W. H. Murray, J. M. Dent, 1951. The last of the classic routes on Garbh Bheinn in the pre-pegging days!

3

Ardnamurchan

Beinn Hiant, 1731 ft. (537632)
Beinn na Seilg, 1123 ft. (456642)
Maps: One-inch Ordnance Survey, 7th Series, Sheet 45. Half-inch Bartholomew latest
   edition, Sheet 50.

Ardnamurchan is usually taken to be the long peninsula north of Loch
Sunart and west of the Salen–Acharacle road. And the definition is
convenient for the purposes of this Guide.

It is served by a road along the southern, or Loch Sunart, side
which leaves something to be desired as a quick access to the area as it
is narrow, winding and full of blind corners. Indeed the driver might
well be excused from further activity during the day to prepare him
for the return journey and this should on no account coincide with
the day of the Strontian Show! In fact this means that the hills are
best visited if one is staying in, or near, the area.

Not that there are any high hills, but they are nonetheless interesting. As far west as the Loch Mudle valley they are made out of metamorphic rock and really comprise an area of high, craggy moorland.
Ben Laga (1679 ft.) is the highest in this ground and is defended on
the main road side by an almost impenetrable screen of Forestry
plantings. Beyond the Loch Mudle, however, the country is more
open and is made up of the remnants of the old 'Central Volcano'
described in the section on Geology in the Introduction. What is
left represents the roots of this structure and there the formerly
molten gabbros and dolerites are arranged in the curious concentric
manner common to 'ring complexes' in various parts of the world.
The features are similar, for instance, to some of these found in the
other Tertiary volcanic centres of Rhum, the Cuillin, Slieve Gullion
and, in part, north Arran and in fact Ardnamurchan is world-famous
as a demonstration area. The circular structure is quite apparent if one

stands in the centre of the last phase of the volcanic activity. This is a rather insignificant little hump situated about midway between Achnaha and Glendrian. It lies in the middle of a plain, about two and a quarter miles in diameter, surrounded on all sides but one by craggy gabbro hills, the only gap through which is the valley of the Allt Sanna to the north-west.

There is a fair amount of bare rock about on the Ardnamurchan hills and in the 'volcanic' country to the west it often crops out in short, steep gabbro or dolerite cliffs which can provide some good scrambles, or even something better as on Beinn na Seilg or Meall nan Con.

Mingarry Castle, about a mile east of Kilchoan Pier, is an interesting ruin. Its origins are obscure, but obviously was a strong point overlooking the Sound of Mull in the days when seaborne transport was easier than the rough inland tracks. Probably it belonged to one of the McIain Lords of the Isles. James IV visited it in 1495, so it must have been a well known keep by that time. Colkitto Mac-Donald, in support of Montrose and Charles I, took the castle in 1644 from the Campbells who were then in possession. This time he only burnt the gate to force entry and the Castle remained habitable for many years afterwards.

There are magnificent sandy beaches around Sanna which form a major tourist attraction to encourage climber-delaying traffic on the road and even at Easter the ground is usually alive with student field parties looking at the geology.

The Point of Ardnamurchan is the most westerly point of the mainland of Great Britain, being about twenty miles west of the longitude of Land's End. There is a road to the Lighthouse at the point, but an attractive alternative is to go on foot round the coast from Sanna.

Possibly the only hills which possess sufficient interest to attract the mountaineer are Ben Hiant and Beinn na Seilg.

Ben Hiant, 1731 ft. – This hill stands on the south coast about 3 miles east from Kilchoan, and rises up steeply from the shore of Loch Sunart, from a prominent headland called Maclean's Nose. There are some steep rocks on the north-east face of the summit, but generally the hill is a grassy one. It can be climbed from the main road south of Loch Mudle, but is most often approached from Kilchoan from where the walk to the top of the hill should take about a couple of hours. The Salen road should be followed for a mile and a half from the hotel to the side of the Allt Choire Mhuilinn, where a small footbridge will be found crossing the stream. From the footbridge make for the western shoulder of Beinn na h-Urchrach, cross it at a convenient point, and then climb up to the summit of Ben Hiant. The view from the top is a fine one, as the hill stands well to the west of the high mountains on the mainland, and extends over the Inner and Outer Isles. The outlook over Loch Sunart is especially fine.

Beinn na Seilg, 1123 ft. – This miniature mountain is a very shapely peak, standing 2 miles west from Kilchoan. It is undoubtedly the most interesting hill on the peninsula. It consists of gabbro, and when climbing it one might almost imagine that one was in Skye. The rock is excellent and offers plenty of scope for pleasant climbing, and several short rock-climbs have been made on the hill in recent years. The most convenient route of ascent is to climb up the hillside from Ormsaigmore to the Lochain Ghleann Locha (*c.* 650 ft.) and then go straight up to the top by an easy slope. The crags make up a vertical face about 100 to 150 ft. high, running along the western side of the little peak to the north of the main top and terminate at the south end with a steep buttress.

Beinn na Seilg has the distinction of being the most westerly thousand-foot hill on the mainland of Great Britain. It may be a miniature mountain, but there is nothing small about the view from it, which is much finer than that from Ben Hiant, as there is nothing of greater height between it and the shores of the Atlantic. Both hills should if possible be climbed, but if there is only time for one, then do Beinn na Seilg.

Paths

Kilmory to Acharacle: Quite a worthwhile two-car walk is along the north coast from the road end at Ockle, east of Kilmory, to Acharacle by the hill path shown on the map. The coastal scenery and the view to the Inner Hebrides is attractive in the first section. From Gortenfearn to Gorteneorn the track goes through new plantings and is uninteresting.

References

Mingarry – Key to the West, Hugo B. Miller. *Scots Magazine,* November 1971.
Scotland: The Tertiary Volcanic Districts, see General Bibliography, p. 28.

4

Moidart

Beinn Odhar Mhor, 2854 ft. (851791)
Beinn Odhar Bheag, 2895 ft. (846778)
Rois-bheinn, 2895 ft. (756778)
Sgurr na Ba Glaise, 2817 ft. (771776)
An t-Slat-bheinn, 2701 ft. (783779)
Druim Fiaclach, 2852 ft. (791792)
An Stac, *c.* 2550 ft. (763793)

Maps: One-inch Ordnance Survey, 7th Series, Sheets 34, 35, 45, 46. Half-inch Bartholomew latest edition, Sheet 50.

Moidart is the district lying to the west of Loch Shiel, south of Loch Eilt and Loch Ailort, and separated from Ardnamurchan by the River Shiel. The northern part of the district is very mountainous and contains two striking groups, namely, Rois-bheinn and the Beinn Odhars.

Formerly rather isolated, the area has now been made much more accessible by the construction of a fast road from Kinlochailort to Kinlochmoidart. With its continuation by the former road from Kinlochmoidart to Acharacle the area is now encircled by a reasonable to very good highway and makes an excellent tourist circuit.

The country now opened up is scenically quite attractive. First, of course there is Loch Shiel which with its 18-mile length is one of the longest and narrowest lochs in Scotland. The view of the loch from Glenfinnan is justly famous, the sheet of water with its pine-tree clad island being symmetrically framed by the two fine-looking peaks of Sgurr Ghuibhsachain and Beinn Odhar. The surface of the loch is only twelve feet above sea level and it is separated from Loch Eil by a watershed which is only about forty feet higher. So that were the land to be submerged by about fifty feet, as is geologically likely, the whole of the district south of Loch Eil would become a large and extremely complicated island. Loch Eilt on the northern margin of the district is three and a half miles long, and is almost cut in two near its eastern end by the delta of the Allt a' Choire Bhuidhe, which has been noticeably growing bigger over the not-too-many years since the author first saw it. The loch is well placed in a wild, steep mountainous setting.

Loch Ailort is a sea loch, although landlocked at its upper end. This feature has aided the development of a fish-farm for rainbow trout whose buildings lie close to the road seen after crossing the River Ailort. The views from the new road along the loch side, while quite pleasant, are not to be compared with those along the Kinlochailort–Mallaig road, but on the other hand once Glen Uig hill is passed there are some excellent views of the surprisingly wooded shores of Loch Moidart and of Eilean Shona.

Between Kinlochmoidart and Acharacle there are one or two rather fine glimpses of Loch Shiel and Ben Resipol, best appreciated if the road is followed in the reverse direction, that is, from Acharacle.

The rocks of the district are all metamorphic types and the new road cuttings show some remarkable geological features. The Mallaig–Kinlochailort section is described in Chapter 5. Near Alisary on Loch Ailort side a quarry shows well black dykes of igneous rock cutting the folded psammitic granulite. Rusty brown dykes of a different sort lie in cuttings between Roshven and Glen Uig while folded strata are well seen along Loch Moidart side, in places seamed with thin, brilliant-white. quartz veins.

Seventeen days after his landing on the mainland of Scotland Prince Charles Edward Stuart shifted his headquarters from Borrodale on Loch nan Uamh (see Chapter 5) to Kinlochmoidart. After a further week making plans he set out on the 18th August, 1745, for the meeting place with his supporters at Glenfinnan, first by walking to Dalilea, probably more or less along the line of the present road and then by boat up Loch Shiel. He spent one night at Glenaladale, on the west side of the loch.

Less well known to history is the castle at Dorlinn – Castle Tioram or Tirrim. This is a 14th Century building of the MacDonalds of Clanranald and survived until 1715 when it was burned by the owner himself before setting out in support of James' uprising. He believed he would not return and did not wish the castle to pass to alien hands. He was right. He was killed at the Battle of Sheriffmuir! The castle is in a delightful setting and is well worth a visit. If you have a boat, be careful of the current in the loch here – the tide makes and ebbs very fast.

Beinn Odhar Mhor, 2854 ft., **Beinn Odhar Bheag,** 2895 ft. – This very fine pair of mountains stand on the north-west side of the upper part of Loch Shiel, 3½ miles south-west from Glenfinnan. Notwithstanding its comparatively low height, the group is one of the most picturesque in the Highlands. As seen from the east near Corpach it dominates the horizon beyond the western end of Loch Eil, and when flecked with snow gullies and slopes, as it is in early spring, it looks much higher than it really is.

Beinn Odhar Mhor is the one more usually ascended, and it is the bigger in bulk, although 41 ft. lower than its partner. It is most easily climbed from a point on the main road about 3 miles west from Glenfinnan, where the Allt a' Ghiubhais crosses under the railway. Go up beside the stream to its eastern tributary which can either be followed up a narrow gorge, or either of its bounding ridges taken. In snow the headwall of Coire Odhar might give some easy gully climbs.

Other and more interesting routes to the mountain can obviously be found, for instance that direct from the filling station at Glenfinnan by way of Lochan nan Sleubhaich. Unfortunately there is at present no bridge over the Abhainn Shlatach at the start of this route and low water is needed. The alternative in wet conditions involves a long detour over rough ground from a (private) bridge near Loch Shiel jetty. The route, however, is most attractive, especially on the ascent. The way to the Beinn Odhars along the loch side should be avoided as timber-felling operations have made it hard going.

The prominent buttresses on the west side of Beinn Odhar Mhor are of good rock and one has given an excellent rock climb (see Appendix II).

Beinn Odhar Bheag stands seven-eighths of a mile S.S.W. of the other, and the walk to it from the first summit is very pleasant. The best parts, and the finest parts of the whole mountain, are the great rock faces at the head of Coire nan Clach and on the south-east face of the peak. The principal features of the two mountains are the great slopes overlooking Loch Shiel, the glaciated rocks on most of the slopes, particularly on the north-east slopes of Beinn Odhar Mhor, and, of course, the magnificent views of the greater part of Loch Shiel to be seen from the summits.

Rois-bheinn, 2895 ft., **Druim Fiaclach,** 2852 ft. – These are the highest points at the west and east ends of the imposing range of hills which stand on the south-east side of Loch Ailort. They are about three miles apart, and the intermediate summits are Sgurr na

Ba Glaise (2817 ft.) and An t-Slat-bheinn (2701 ft.). The fifth summit of the group is An Stac (*c.* 2550 ft.), which is an outlying peak standing about 1 mile to the north of the western part of the main ridge. The hills are of the grassy craggy nature so characteristic of the Western Highlands, but the north-west side of Sgurr na Ba Glaise and the south face of Druim Fiaclach are very rocky. An Stac is a very steep, rounded, conical hill, and it and Rois-bheinn itself are the most conspicuous members of the group, as seen from the west. Druim Fiaclach is, however, the finest individual mountain, as, in addition to its precipitous southern face, three well-defined ridges radiate from the summit, running S.W., N., and E.S.E. The last ridge, as seen from the north, seems to have a number of small teeth, and from them the hill doubtless has its name. This ridge, while narrow, presents no difficulty and ends in a knob overlooking the inner recesses of Glen Aladale.

Given clear weather, the best way to climb these hills is from east to west, like most of the west-coast hills, as the grand views to the west are always in front, culminating in that from Rois-bheinn itself.

Owing to the tangle of small foothills and streams at the head of Loch Ailort some time may easily be lost in hitting off the best route to Druim Fiaclach.

Take the track which passes north of the entrance to Glenshian Hotel by some outhouses. Continue through assorted relics of war-time habitations until way can be made over rather wet ground to the little glen which runs south of the wooded knoll (Tom Odhar) which is a prominent feature on the left. The beginning of a good footpath will be found here leading up the small glen. Follow this path up on to the open hillside to a height of about 400 ft. beside a small dell containing hollies and birches, and then traverse across the hillside in a south-east direction to the Allt a' Bhuiridh. Cross it and climb up the steep grassy north-west slope of Druim Fiaclach so as to hit the north ridge, and so on to the summit, which is rocky, and is sur-mounted by a well-built cairn. From Glenshian Hotel one may of course follow the left bank of the Allt an t' Sagairt but the route is pretty rough up the gorge of the stream, which contains some fine waterfalls.

The ridge leading south-west from the summit of Druim Fiaclach is quite broad, with precipitous rocks on the south side overhanging Coire Reidh, and leads to the west top of Druim Fiaclach (2769 ft.) There is then a steep rocky descent south to the bealach at the head of

8. Garbh Bheinn of Ardgour. The Great Ridge (left) bounded on the right by the Great Gully, Pinnacle Ridge on the right.

9. Garbh Bheinn, Ardgour. The great Gully cleaves the buttress below the summit, with the Great Ridge on the left. The top of Pinnacle Ridge forms the pointed middle peak, with the North-East Buttress beyond. *D. McKellar.*

10. Ben Resipol from Garbh Bheinn. Loch Sunart behind climbers: Ben Hiant (Ardnamurchan) above. Rhum and Eigg to the right.

11. Sgurr Dhomhnuill from Strontian Glen.

Coire Reidh (*c.* 2450 ft.) followed by a grassy ascent to the top of An t-Slat-bheinn, and thence to the foot of the steep eastern face of Sgurr na Ba Glaise, the final climb up which is over steep grass and rock. This peak has some very steep rocks on its north-west face. From the summit an easy descent leads down to the wide and grassy Bealach an Fhiona (2346 ft.)

From the bealach there is a steep stony ascent to the east top of Rois-bheinn (2887 ft.), which has no cairn and from which a grassy walk of three-eighths of a mile leads to the west top (2876 ft.). The northern face of Rois-bheinn is steep and rocky. Should one wish to climb An Stac it will probably be best to retrace one's steps to near the bealach, and then make north for its summit, and descend its north side over Seann Chruach to the path at the back of Tom Odhar.

If other routes to Rois-bheinn are being considered, remember that the Loch Ailort slopes of the hills are being progressively afforested.

Paths

The former track from Kinlochailort to Glen Uig and Kinloch-moidart has now been replaced, and in part obliterated, by the new road. The short stretch from Inverailort Pier to Alisary is still worth following for the views which can be had from it. The former track from Glen Uig to Smearisary is now a road, but is worth walking so that one can return by the coast north of Samalaman House. (Track in part obliterated.)

One can also walk from Kinlochmoidart to Kinlochailort by going up Glen Moidart by track to Assary and up over the Bealach Fhiona to Coir' a' Bhuiridh and down to Glenshian Hotel by the Tom Odhar path already mentioned.

5

Locheil and Morar

Beinn Bhan, 2613 ft. (141858)
Culvain, 3224 ft. (003876)
Streap Comhlaidh, 2916 ft. (954860)
Streap, 2988 ft. (946864)
Sgurr Thuilm, 3164 ft. (939879)
Sgurr nan Coireachan, 3136 ft. (903880)
Sgurr an Utha, 2610 ft. (885839)
Carn a' Ghobhair, 1794 ft. (717964)
Sgurr an Eilein Ghiubhais, 1713 ft. (727973)
Sgurr Bhuidhe, 1433 ft. (722947)

Munro's Tables, Section 7.

Maps: One-inch Ordnance Survey, 7th Series, Sheets 34, 35. Half-inch Bartholomew latest edition, Sheet 50.

The great through-valley in which lie Loch Eil and Loch Eilt, with its northern counterpart containing Loch Arkaig and Loch Morar define a strip of country which can be divided into two areas of strongly contrasting scenery and mountaineering interest.

East of Gleann Fionnlighe, which runs north from the head of Loch Eil, the rocks belong to the thick group of flaggy psammitic granulites (see p. 19). As these rocks show little variation in resistance to erosion they give rise to rather smooth slopes and ill-defined summits. West of Gleann Fionnlighe the country is made up of diverse schists and gneisses which have been eroded into steep craggy mountains and narrow ridges. Even in the low ground which lies towards the western seaboard, the country is remarkably rugged, with attractive, wild, rocky hillsides set off well against tree-clad lower slopes descending to the shores of the inland lochs and sea inlets. The magnificent beaches around Morar and Arisaig, although of little interest to the climber, provide a wonderful foreground to the views of the mountains of the islands of Rhum and Skye. They are, justly, one of the major tourist attractions of Scotland.

The mountains of the central part of this belt of country are higher than those so far described and culminate in Culvain (3224 ft.). Height is not everything, however, and several of the lower peaks are more attractive to the hill-walker.

The area is served by the main road from Fort William to Mallaig. In the summer this carries an extraordinary amount of traffic and although it is being progressively improved, there are still narrow stretches where hold-ups behind convoys of slow-moving lorries or caravans can be frustrating. Climbers using it should start early and finish late!

The eastern part of the area is yearly becoming more afforested and access to the hills is gradually becoming more difficult. At Annat, on Loch Eil side, the road passes by an immense paper pulp mill for which much of the new timber ultimately will be destined. Unfortunately, with its size and plume of steam, it cannot be said to add much to the former magnificent view eastwards along Loch Eil to Ben Nevis, especially when re-enforced by a huge caravan park on Annat spit. From the caravanners' point of view, of course, the outlook to the west must be one of the finest obtainable from any major Scottish site!

The area is full of historical associations of the 1745 rising. Loch nan Uamh near Arisaig is the place of Prince Charles Edward Stuart's landing on the Scottish mainland on 25th July of that year and likewise the point of departure on his escape to France on 19th September, 1746. A cairn marks the latter place. The Monument of Glenfinnan marks the (arguable) spot of the raising of the Jacobite Standard on 19th August, 1745. (The area is now the property of the National Trust for Scotland with an Information Centre, car park and tea-dispenser.) Achnacarry, at the east end of Loch Arkaig is still the home of the descendants of the 'Gentil Locheil'. A cave near Druimandarroch on Loch nan Uamh was occupied by the Prince in hiding after Culloden, on his return from the Outer Isles and the area is well served with other, more remote, Prince's caves, several of which are authentic. Despite the romanticization of the adventure the basic facts still remain to mark it as one of remarkable daring, loyalty, and personal fortitude, which fits with the wild mountain background better than many tales of fiction. One cannot escape its aura.

Most of the hills described in this chapter can be climbed from the main road. Those which cannot, can be reached from its offshoot up the Great Glen, towards Achnacarry. The Streaps and Sgurr Thuilm can be reached with equal ease (as far as walking distance is concerned) from Strathan at the head of Loch Arkaig. The road access along the loch, however, is slow and time consuming (see Chapter 6) but the writer considers this way of reaching these hills to be scenically preferable to Loch Eil side.

Beinn Bhan, 2612 ft. **Stob a' Ghrianain,** 2420 ft., etc. – The less mountainous eastern part of the region described in this section of the Guide has none the less some worthy hills for a short day, or even a half-day's outing, and they would be more highly thought of if it were not for the more spectacular and higher neighbours to the west.

Gleann Fionnlighe, after running initially northwards from Loch Eil trends north-east, joining over a shallow col (c. 1000 ft.) with Glen Mallie to form a through-valley from Loch Eil to Loch Arkaig. To the east lies another similar curving through-valley, that of Gleann Suileag–Glen Loy. The ridge between the two valleys contains a number of fairly well isolated, although well rounded, hills. Of these Beinn Bhan at the east end of the chain above the Great Glen and Aodann Chleirig (2150 ft.) above Kinlocheil are both worth a visit for the magnificent views they provide of Ben Nevis and its attendant mountains. If one is chosen it should be Beinn Bhan with its additional views up Glen Spean and the Great Glen. Coire Bhotrais on its northern side is deep and well-formed but provides no climbing in summer.

Beinn Bhan is best ascended from the Banavie–Gairlochy road, but can also be climbed from Inverskilavulin in Glen Loy. A scrappy gully scramble can be had up the stream beside the forestry fence east of Inverskilavulin but cannot be recommended. Aodann Chleirig and its neighbour Beinn an t'Sneachda are reached easily from Gleann Fionnlighe.

The long ridge south and east of the Gleann Suileag–Glen Loy valley is called by the appropriate name of Druim Fada (Long Ridge) and provides an excellent half-day's walk. Stob a' Ghrianain at its eastern end is an old volcanic neck (rather unusual for Northern Scotland) and is one of the finest viewpoints in the Highlands. It has an unobstructed view of about 200 degrees with a magnificent prospect of Ben Nevis and the Grampians. It is best ascended from Annat, on Loch Eil, although the alternative by way of Puiteachan in Glen Loy is not unattractive.

Culvain, or **Gaor Bheinn,** (3224 ft.) – This rather massive mountain (spelled Gulvain on some maps) stands about 6 miles north of the west end of Loch Eil, and it is the highest of those described in this chapter. It has two summits, the north one being the higher. The most practical approach to the hill is from the south, and the best route is up Gleann Fionnlighe from the bridge on the Fort William–Mallaig road. From the bridge there is a rough road on the east side of the stream for one and a quarter miles, when it crosses over to a place called Wauchan (an appalling Ordnance Survey corruption of the Gaelic 'Uamhachan'). It then follows the west side of the stream, ultimately becoming a mere track, as far as the junction with the Allt a' Choire Reidh. From the latter point one should strike straight up the south shoulder of Culvain, which is a very steep and un-relieved grass slope, to the south top (3148 ft.). From this top it is a very pleasant high-level walk along the crest of the mountain for $\frac{3}{4}$ mile to the north summit. The lowest point on the ridge is about 2827 ft., and shortly before one reaches the foot of the main summit the ridge, which so far has been broad and grassy, becomes quite narrow. There is a big cairn on the summit. On the north-east side of the mountain there is a rather fine glaciated corrie, Coire Screamhach, in which is found a soft rock which the local shepherds used to carve into ornaments.

The rocks on Culvain largely consist of a banded granite, or 'granite-gneiss' and on the west side of the mountain this forms steep slabs, which, though of little interest to the rock climber are best avoided by the hill-walker. Stags shot on this slope are reputed to 'fall right down the mountain'!

Streap, 2988ft., **Streap Comhlaidh,** 2916 ft. – These are the highest points of the series of peaks which one sees to the north-west from near the head of Loch Eil. The group stands between Glen Finnan on the west and Gleann Dubh Lighe on the east. It contains in all five distinct summits, the lowest and most southerly being Beinn an Tuim (2656 ft.) which stands two and a quarter miles N.E. from the head of Loch Shiel. From Beinn an Tuim it is $2\frac{1}{4}$ miles N.N.E. to the highest summit over the 2 intermediate tops of Meall an Uillt Chaoil (2769 ft. not named on the one-inch map) and Stob Coire nan Cearc (2917 ft.), the intervening dips being pretty considerable.

Formerly an attractive way up the Streaps was by Glen Dubh Lighe and a slabby scramble up the east side of Stob Coire nan Cearc to the summit ridge, but active afforestation of the lower part of the glen renders access difficult, with locked gates at the points of path departure. The alternative route is by Glen Finnan and, if this

53

route is taken, note that in times of high water the River Finnan is impossible to cross between Glenfinnan and Corryhully and possibly even well beyond that into the headstreams. In such conditions go over Beinn an Tuim. In dry weather it is a matter of taste where one ascends to the ridge from Glen Finnan, the finest part lying between Bealach Coire nan Cearc and Streap itself. This stretch is pretty narrow in places and in winter requires full mountaineering treatment. Some parties have found that it took longer than they bargained for.

On the west side of Streap the slope descending to Glen Finnan is exceedingly steep, while on its southern face a high corrie, Coire Chuirn, contains the remains of an immense landslip which has detached from the headwall of the corrie along a fault line. Some of the rock on the north side of the corrie is still unstable, as is shown by the yellow scars left by relatively recent rockfalls. The trace of the fault crosses the ridge a few yards south from the summit of the mountain and trends down the Glen Finnan side in a curious easy-angled rake which forms a quick way down towards Corryhully.

Streap Comhlaidh, ½ mile E.S.E. of Streap, is connected to that mountain by a ridge which, near the west end, is quite narrow.

Both mountains can be climbed from Strathan at the head of Loch Arkaig by way of Gleann a' Chaoruinn or Leac na Carnaich. There is a bridge, not shown on the 7th Series map, over the River Pean near Strathan and another, shown on the map, near the confluence of the Allt a' Chaoruinn. The ascent from this side is rather a trudge, although if the route over Leac na Carnaich is taken Streap Comhlaidh appears as a very shapely mountain with an immense curving sweep down to Gleann Camgharaidh.

Sgurr Thuilm, 3164 ft., **Sgurr nan Coireachan,** 3136 ft. – These two hills stand near the head of Glen Finnan, about 5 miles from the Glenfinnan Monument. They are steep and rugged and round of the two of them gives the best day's outing in this section of the Guide. In good weather the route should take in Sgurr Thuilm first as the walk thereafter has fine views to the west and north-west.

From Glenfinnan the road to Glen House is taken as far as the railway viaduct. This is one of the earliest mass concrete structures to be erected in Britain (about 1899) and one of the viaduct pillars is reputed to contain the remains of a horse and cart which fell down from the top during the construction! Do not cross the bridge to Glen House but keep up the track on the west side of Glen Finnan. The meander flats of the river tend to be marshy and the track is often very wet after the initial mile or so, especially where minor side-streams fan out from the hill slopes above. Near Corryhully it improves once more. Beyond Corryhully the path is not shown on the one-inch map but is still well-defined as far as the fork in the river south of Druim Coir' a' Bheithe. From the fork climb steeply, but easily, up the Druim to the summit of Sgurr Thuilm on which there is a smallish cairn. Turning westwards, a pleasant walk with fine views takes one over the intermediate top of Beinn Garbh (2716 ft.) and Meall nan Tarmachain (2708 ft.) to the summit of Sgurr nan Coireachan on which there is a big cairn. The descent can then be made south-eastwards over Sgurr a' Choire Riabhaich (2718 ft.). On the previous one-inch maps the height of Sgurr nan Coireachan was given as 3133 ft.

If it is decided to go round in the reverse order the path in the glen should be left about ½ mile beyond Corryhully, near the point where the path dips down to the stream. From here a good stalker's path strikes up to the left and leads one easily up the south-east shoulder of Sgurr a' Choire Riabhaich to a height of about 1250 ft.

The corries of the group are wild and rocky, especially Coire Carnaig, north of Corryhully and Coire Chaisil and Coire Dhuibh north of the Sgurr Thuilm–Beinn Garbh ridge. There are some cliffs in the latter corrie and also on the west side of Coire Thollaidh. While they might give short routes with the use of artificial aids the climbs would be rather pointless. The apparent steep slabs in Coire Chaisil, as seen from Strathan, are easy-angled.

Sgurr an Utha, 2610 ft. **Sgurr a' Mhuidhe,** 1838 ft., etc. – North of the Glenfinnan–Loch Ailort road the hills are exceptionally craggy, but none offer much mountaineering interest. Loch Beoraid, which lies north of this rocky ridge is deep-set and narrow and is worth a visit by way of the Feith a' Chatha (reached from the 'Cross' about 1½ miles west from Glenfinnan or by the path to Meoble from Arienskill – see below). Good views of the loch can also be had from Sgurr an Utha (also reached easily from the 'Cross' by way of the glaciated slabs on the north side of the Allt an Utha). Sgurr a' Mhuidhe, on the west side of the Allt Feith a' Chatha has even more bare rock, but set at an easy angle.

There are often eagles to be seen hereabouts, and on one occasion the author's colleague was 'de-hatted' by one appearing suddenly out of the mist.

North of Loch Beoraid the country is wild, inaccessible and, to the author, not very attractive. If coming from the head of Loch Morar, however, the ridge from Sgurr an Ursainn over Beinn Garbh is a worthy addition to Sgurr nan Coireachan–Sgurr Thuilm traverse. There is also a good path from the watershed between Glen an Obain Bhig and Glen Pean to the col west of Sgurr nan Coireachan, if a shorter route is desired. The path is not shown on the one-inch map. Glen an Obain Bhig (not named on the one-inch map but the Loch of that name is shown) is an impressive place. Wild goats can often be seen there and also in Glen Toadail which lies on the south side of Loch Morar a mile or so west of Oban:

Carn a' Ghobhair, 1794 ft., **Sgurr an Eilein Ghiubhais,** 1713 ft., **Sgurr Bhuidhe,** 1433 ft. – These small hills stand about 3 miles east of Mallaig, and they are well worth a visit from anyone who has a spare day there, on account of the magnificent views to be had from the summits. The steep drop of 1713 ft. from the top of Sgurr an Eilein Ghiubhais to the shore of Loch Nevis (in 2250 ft. horizontal) is very impressive. There is a very steep cliff about 200 ft. high on the south side of Sgurr Bhuidhe which unconfirmed rumour says has provided some climbing.

Walks and Paths

Fassfern to the Great Glen: This walk through Gleann Suileag and Glen Loy can be done in half a day. It has little scenic merit but serves to pass the time if the weather is poor and two car-borne parties can swap keys. Take the path from the gate on the east side of the Allt Suileag bridge (now a forestry track) and follow through to join the Glen Loy road at Achanellan, crossing the Suileag to the north bank at Glensuileag bothy. The part across the watershed is not well defined. A point of interest is the remnants of several old charcoal hearths on the hillside about 1½ miles north of Fassfern. It is possible that iron was smelted here at one time.

Fassfern House was the resting place of Prince Charles Edward on the third night after raising the Standard at Glenfinnan.

Kinlocheil to Achnacarry: This longer route through the hills is at least a full day trip and is scenically much to be preferred to the one just described. It has good views in Glen Fionnlighe and Glen Mallie. The route is obvious from the one-inch map, the section across the watershed being trackless. Two shorter variants are available at the time of writing, but may be obliterated as forestry proceeds. The first is to do a short circuit up Glen Fionnlighe to the Allt a'Choire Reidhe, thence by the path shown on the map across the bealach south of Meall Onfhaidh and down Gleann Suileag. The second is to reach Glen Mallie by way of Glen Loy and a path north from Achnanellan over the Mam. The walk down Glen Mallie to Achnacarry is most attractive, with excellent views of the Beinn Bhan corries and of Loch Arkaig, on whose island the osprey once nested.

Kinlochailort to Loch Beoraid and Loch Morar: This is the access path to Meoble Lodge from the west end of Loch Eilt and is shown on the one-inch map just north of Arienskill. It has no continuation beyond Loch Morar side, the Lodge being serviced by boat. Any further progress, east or west, is hard going. Nevertheless walkers may wish to use it to visit Loch Beoraid, and a round trip is possible by returning along the north side of the loch to Kinlochbeoraid, thence south by a steep trackless ascent to the Feith a' Chatha and the 'Cross' on the main road west of Glenfinnan. Alternatively continue on east by the extraordinarily narrow glen of the Allt a' Chaol–Ghlinne to Glen Finnan. This walk takes one into some wild country.

One can, of course, join up with the Morar–Arkaig paths by following up the Allt a'Choire north east of Kinlochbeoraid over the col west of Sgurr nan Coireachan where there is an unmapped path (see p. 56) to Gleann an Obain Bhig.

The Great Glen: The tow-path of the Caledonian Canal can be walked from Banavie Locks to Gairlochy. In good weather there are fine views to Ben Nevis and up the Great Glen. The walk can be shortened by passing under the canal to the Banavie–Achnacarry road either at Glen Loy or at the Allt Laragain. Near the mouth of the latter stream lies Tor Castle, on the banks of the River Lochy. It is ruinous, but in a fine situation. Permission to visit it would be necessary as it lies in private ground. It is traditionally the home of Banquo, if he ever existed. It has a long history extending, possibly, from the time of the Scots of Dalriada up until the '45 when it finally was abandoned. It is likely that several castles were built upon the site and one of the author's colleagues has found fragments of vitrified fort there. The present ruins probably are those of a fourteenth-century structure.

The Mallaig Road: The new rock cuttings between the railway bridge $1\frac{1}{2}$ miles east of Glenfinnan and Kinlochailort show wonderful sections in the metamorphic rocks. In places these have an interest beyond their geological significance and are worth a minute or two of anyone's time.

From the bridge to the deep cutting just east of Glenfinnan itself the rock is granite gneiss and is highly ornamental, being pale grey with black wisps (mica) and having curious, contorted pods and lenses of white granite pegmatite. It makes a nice rockery ornament. The deep cutting itself shows some remarkable folds in granulite. Beyond Glenfinnan and right on to Kinlochailort there are mica schists and striped schists, more or less shot through with streaks of granite pegmatite. One interesting locality is worth a visit. Just west of the Allt a'Ghuibhais, about 3 miles west of Glenfinnan, a steep rock face shows fine sections of huge, white pegmatite veins with lustrous plates of silvery mica. On the hillside above and to the west, a curious flat slab, several hundreds of feet across shows what is probably the most crumpled and folded rock to be seen in the area. It seems hardly possible for rock to have attained the fantastic shapes displayed there. There is also an excellent view from here westwards along Loch Eilt. (Photo 18.)

The wonderful coastal scenery west from Loch nan Uamh has already been mentioned, as has the Prince's Cave at Druimandarroch near Arisaig. A more mundane but nevertheless interesting feature is the railway bridge at Borrodale which in its time (1899) caused quite a stir in engineering circles because of its daring use of mass concrete over what was then an unprecedented span. In fact it was the first concrete *railway* bridge ever built.

6

Loch Arkaig and Glen Dessarry

Meall na Teanga, *c.* 3012 ft. (220923)
Sron a' Choire Ghairbh, 3066 ft. (222946)
Ben Tee, 2957 ft. (241973)
Fraoch Bheinn, 2808 ft. (986840)
Sgurr Mor, 3290 ft. (966980)
Sgurr nan Coireachan, 3125 ft. (934957)
Sgurr na Ciche, 3410 ft. (903967)
Carn Mor, 2718 ft. (904910)
Sgurr na h-Aide, 2818 ft. (882932)

Munro's Tables, section 7.

Maps: One-inch Ordnance Survey, 7th Series, Sheets 35, 36. Half-inch Bartholomew latest edition, Sheet 50.

Note: In this chapter, *Glen Dessarry, Glendessary,* and *Glendessarry* are deliberate variations because of Ordnance usage.

The area described in this chapter lies between the Loch Arkaig–Glen Pean–Loch Morar valley and the Glen Garry–Loch Quoich–Loch Nevis depression. All the hills in this section can best be approached from the south or Arkaig–Morar side or from the Great Glen, with the exception of Gairich and Ben Aden which, as they are best reached from Glen Garry will be described in the next chapter.

North of Loch Arkaig the hills, as will be seen from the geological map (p. 19) are made up largely of the granulite rock and so are smoother and less rugged than those to the west. None the less they contain some very fine mountains which are certainly more attractive then their counterparts to the south. These are the *Clunes Hills* at the east end of Loch Arkaig. The *Glen Dessarry Hills* which lie beyond the west end of that loch make up part of the rugged, mountainous country known as the Rough Bounds, and like the mountains to the south, are made up of schists and gneisses, shot through, in many places by innumerable glistening white veins of granite pegmatite. Between these two mountain groups, the watershed north of Loch

Arkaig is a high tract of grass and peat out of which rise several size-able, but on the whole rather uninteresting hills. For the purposes of description they are included with the Clunes group.

Like the area to the south, the district has many historical associations. There is a genuine Prince's cave (which the author has never been able to find!) above Achnacarry at the east end of Loch Arkaig where he spent some time after his escape from Culloden. From there he passed along Loch Arkaig side on his way to the Isles, passing through the narrow defile of Glen Pean on 17th–18th April, 1746. The Prince once more passed by Achnacarry on his wanderings after his return from the Hebrides. On 20th July he crossed from Glen Dessarry to Loch Quoich, probably over one of the passes north of the present lodge. There is a local rumour that the war-chest of the insurgent army – 4000 Louis d'Or – still lies buried as the Loch Arkaig Treasure somewhere near Caonich. Despite diligent search over many camping evenings in the neighbourhood, the author and his colleagues failed to confirm its presence!

A short distance west of the end of Loch Arkaig the road passes a ruin on the left. This is the 'Barracks' – the local name given to the post of the 'Moving Patrol' – a kind of watch placed on the Glens after the '45. Evidently several such posts were established in the narrows of the western glens and the watch would pass from one to the other on irregular beats. Conditions must have been like those of the N.W. Frontier in later days!

More recently, however, the area was the centre of Commando training during the last war. Achnacarry House was the headquarters and from it courses were organized in all weathers through the adjacent country. Foundations of dummy assault craft can still be seen beside the Achnacarry road. It was thought proper that the deeds of these brave men should be remembered by a memorial at their training ground, but as Achnacarry is on a dead-end road it was hardly the place for many to see it. Instead, the Commando Memorial was placed above Spean Bridge at the junction of the main Great Glen road and the branch to Achnacarry. The situation is magnificent and the triple figures of the statuary are impressive, in all making a worthy tribute to their exploits and sacrifices. It is perhaps not out of place here to recall that some of them were members of the S.M.C.

The main access to the hills is, of course, by the public road from Spean Bridge to Fort William, by way of Gairlochy, to the head of

Loch Arkaig. The road along the loch side is very slow and winding and from its end a rough – in places very rough – private estate road leads on past Strathan as far as Glendessary Lodge. At the time of writing, permission to take cars along this road is usually obtainable except during the stalking season, but there is no vehicular right-of-way. On some small-scale maps it is implied that the road continues to Morar. This is emphatically not the case! From Strathan or Glendessary Lodge fairish tracks lead on up the main glens. (See 'Paths' at the end of this chapter.)

Access to several of the hills can be had from the Glen Garry side. The public road to Kinloch Hourn is useful as far as the point where it leaves the Quoich Reservoir to follow the pass over to Kinloch Hourn. From that point onwards only foot access is possible, as the enlargement of Loch Quoich has inundated the former road to Kinlochquoich Lodge.

The Clunes Hills can be approached from Kilfinnan, near Laggan Locks, in the Great Glen.

The most westerly of the hills described in this chapter can easily be reached by boat by way of Lochs Nevis or Morar. There is no regular service but arrangements for private hire can usually be made at Mallaig (see p. 73).

Many of the mountains in the west are pretty inaccessible to climbers coming by car or boat from the main centres of tourist accommodation, and involve long day outings to do more than one or two peaks. It is best to camp, and the situations in the remote glens are truly wonderful when the weather is fine. The chances of good weather are not high in the summer months however and over many years the author's experience is that rain falls there *on average* about one day in two. Even in summer the wind can be high in the passes and good equipment is necessary. For instance at Kinlochmorar one night late in May three out of five tents of the author's survey team were torn to ribbons, while the loch itself was almost obliterated under a haze of spindrift. The gale was about force 10.

Camping in the lower glens is restricted. Permission to camp along Loch Arkaig side must be obtained at Bunarkaig or Clunes but is readily granted on payment of a small fee. There are caravans in secluded sites and also cottages which can be hired from Locheil Estates, c/o West Highland Estates, High Street, Fort William. Camping is forbidden by notices painted on the rocks at several places along Loch Quoich, but can be arranged at Kinloch Hourn, which is not too far from the Quoich-side access to several of the hills described in this chapter.

THE CLUNES HILLS

Sron a' Choire Ghairbh, 3066 ft. **Meall na Teanga,** *c.* 3012 ft. – These two mountains can be reached easily from Clunes on the Loch Arkaig road. From Clunes continue along the road through the Dark Mile to the Eas Chia-aig (the 'waterfall' on the O.S. map just north of the east end of the Loch). Go up by a rough path on the east bank of the fall. This track is followed for about 1½ miles through Forestry Commission plantings until they thin out and a way can be made up to the right over Meall Breac to Meall Odhar. From the latter hill a pleasant high-level walk takes one eastwards along the ridge to the summit of Meall Coire Lochan (2971 ft.), thence descends by a sharp little ridge to a saddle, and up a broad stony ridge to the top of Meall na Teanga. Continuing along the northern ridge of the latter for about a mile brings one to the bealach (*c.* 1990 ft.) at the head of the Allt Glas Dhoire, from which there is a good path to near the top of Sron a' Choire Ghairbh. On the return journey a pleasant variation can be made, after the bealach is reached, by following a path which runs down the north side of the Allt Glas Dhoire and thence through the forest towards Loch Lochy. Forestry access roads lead back to Clunes.

If coming from Kilfinnan Farm strike up steep slopes to the top of Meall nan Dearcag (2262 ft.) and from it a walk with good views leads along the broad eastern ridge of Sron a' Choire Ghairbh.

Ben Tee, 2957 ft. – This hill can be climbed from Laggan Locks by way of the Kilfinnan Burn. (Keep high on the north bank until above the waterfall.)

From Kilfinnan the round of Sron a' Choire Ghairbh and Ben Tee makes a very fine outing, with excellent views up Glen Garry and along the Great Glen.

Geal Charn 2636 ft., is easily climbed from Achnasaul on Loch Arkaig side. It has some rather good views towards Meall na Teanga, but is otherwise undistinguished.

On the watershed ridge between Loch Arkaig and Glen Garry **Sgurr Choinnich,** 2450 ft. and **Meall Blair** 2153 ft. have quite respectable corries on their northern sides. **Sgurr Mhurlagain,** 2885 ft. is the culminating point of a group of ridges which enclose corries on the Glen Kingie side. All these hills are rather uninteresting if approached from Loch Arkaig but are most easily ascended therefrom. **Fraoch Bheinn,** 2808 ft. is a rather fine mountain, isolated from both the watershed ridge and the Glen Dessary group by two deep bealachs which provide easy access from Loch Arkaig to Glen Kingie. The more westerly of these – the Feith a' Chicheanais – the easier and lower, and is used as access to Sgurr Mor (q.v.). The north ridge of Fraoch Bheinn is narrow and should be interesting in winter. It is reached by traversing the eastern pass – the Dearg Allt – from Strathan at the head of Loch Arkaig.

THE GLEN DESSARRY HILLS

The Glen Dessarry Hills comprise some of the wildest scenery on the Scottish mainland. They are traversed by two main and one subsidiary valley, all of which are steep-sided and narrow-bottomed. Glen Pean, the most southerly of the three, has virtually no floor in places, with steep, craggy hillsides rising either directly from the river bank or from the shore of the remote Loch Leum am t-Sagairt ('Loch of the Priest's Jump' – the story is not known locally). Glen Pean is the pass between Loch Arkaig and Loch Morar. The other main valley leading from Loch Arkaig to Loch Nevis, comprises Glen Dessarry and the Mam na Cloich 'Airde. It is less narrow than Glen Pean, but has rock scenery on a grander scale. Gleann an Lochain Eanaiche, the subsidiary valley, leads from Glen Dessarry to Loch Morar. These valleys, together with Glen Kingie and Loch Quoich, isolate three ridges of which the one between Glen Dessarry, Glen Kingie and Loch Quoich is by far the most interesting to mountaineers. It is about 6 miles long, including in its course three major summits over 3000 ft. and never falling below a level of about 2200 ft.

The slopes determining the ridges of the Glen Dessarry Hills are frequently very steep, consisting of crags interspersed with grassy ledges. In general, the direct descent to the valleys from all the main peaks, especially in mist or under winter conditions, requires more care in the choice of a suitable line than is usual for Scottish hills outwith the rock-climbing areas. One tends to get involved with steep rock outcrops through which the best route is not always apparent.

Carn Mor, 2718 ft. – This is the western and culminating point of long, undulating ridge which stretches westwards from Monadh Gorm above the west end of Loch Arkaig. It lies between Glen Pean on the south and the Dessarry-Eanaiche pass on the north. From Strathan, the ridge can be followed easily throughout, but is rather monotonous until the rise to Carn Mor itself is reached. The most pleasant route of ascent is from Upper Glendessarry by way of Coir' an Eich or its boundary slopes. There are fine views down Loch Morar from the summit of the mountain. If it is intended to return by Glen Pean it is worth noting that the southern slopes of Carn Mor, apart from being very steep in places, are much cut up by landslip fissures, especially on the less steep ground between the summit and Loch Leum an t'Sagairt. Some of these are narrow and might not easily be seen when the snow is lying. Several are quite deep.

Over a roughly oval area between Upper Glendessarry and Glen Pean Cottage (ruin) the compass can be quite inaccurate; in practice this is not likely to be troublesome unless it is held close to, or steadied on, the rocks.

Sgurr na h'Aide, 2818 ft. – This is the very striking hill seen from several points on the way up Loch Arkaig apparently at the head of the loch. It is frequently mistaken for Sgurr na Ciche. The hill is the culminating point of the ridge between Gleann an Lochain Eanaiche and the Mam na Cloich' Airde and can be easily ascended from the head of Loch Nevis, from which it is only $1\frac{1}{2}$ miles distant. It can also be ascended by a very entertaining route over Meall na Sroine, the eastern end of the ridge. There are two summits, connected by a ridge which in places is quite narrow. The Ordnance Survey only acknowledges one – the western one – as the true summit and omits details of height for the eastern one, which looks at least as high! The direct descent to Gleann an Lochain Eanaiche needs especial care, as it runs into an area of steep boiler-plate slabs.

The Sgurr Mor-Sgurr na Ciche Ridge – It is of course this ridge which forms the main attraction to climbers visiting the district and, indeed, it must be counted amongst the finest in the country. Not only is it narrow enough in places to provide a genuine 'mountaineering' atmosphere – in hard winter conditions it demands care in the section between An Eag and Sgurr na Ciche but its traverse takes one through scenery of considerable diversity. Sgurr Mor, although fairly steep-sided and narrow, is a predominantly grassy hill, but as the ridge is followed to the west the rock scenery becomes very impressive, with deep corries and slabby slopes. If the ridge is to be traversed it is strongly recommended that it should be followed from east to west, as in this direction both the scenery and the elevation culminate in Sgurr na Ciche.

The summits of the ridge in order from east to west are as follows: Sgurr an Fhuarain (2957 ft.); Sgurr Mor (3290 ft.); Sgurr Beag (2890

12. Sgurr Ghiubhsachain and Loch Shiel.

13. Ben Hiant and Mingarry Castle.

14. Meall nan Con, Ardnamurchan. Gabbro cliffs, 50 ft. to 100 ft. high, which give some scrambling. *Inst. Geol. Sciences*

15. Rhum and Eigg from Ardnamurchan. Skye on right.

16. The Moidart Hills Rois-bheinn in cloud, Sgurr na Ba Glaise (centre), An Stac and Druim Fiaclach. View looking south-east over Loch nan Uamh.

17. Loch Ailort, An Stac and Rois-bheinn (in cloud).

ft.); An Eag (2856 ft.); Sgurr nan Coireachan (3125 ft.); Garbh Chioch Beag (six-inch map, no elevation given); Garbh Chioch Beag (c. 3365 ft.); Sgurr na Ciche (3410 ft.).

The summits from Sgurr an Fhuarain to Sgurr Beag of course, make up the north ridge of Glen Kingie and are not strictly Glen Dessarry hills although they are now most easily reached from that glen. The true boundary of the latter runs from Druim a' Chuirn, above Glendessarry Lodge, to join the main ridge at An Eag.

The mountains of the main ridge were formerly readily reached from Kinlochquoich at west end of the natural Loch Quoich but the reservoir now extends well beyond that point. This should be remembered if old accounts are read. While the ascent of all the tops and indeed the traverse of the complete ridge can still be effected from the Glen Garry side by circuiting the head of the reservoir (see p. 80), long walks are involved, which are only practicable in fair weather. In bad weather flooded side streams may be impassable. If a boat can be hired on Loch Quoich, several of the hills could be easily approached by that means, but in recent years all available boats have been booked up by fishing parties. The only certain way of reaching the hills in all conditions is by the Loch Arkaig road and the paths leading on from it.

Sgurr Mor, 3290 ft. – From Glendessary Lodge the route to Sgurr Mor goes over the pass of the Feith a' Chicheanais to Glen Kingie (see p. 68), from whence the ascent of the hill can be made without difficulty. If Sgurr Mor alone is to be climbed, then a convenient route of ascent is by way of a good stalkers' path on the north side of the River Kingie. The path which is shown on the one-inch map at first leads westwards, then ascends in a series of zig-zags to the summit of Sgurr Beag and that mountain can be traversed to Sgurr Mor, or to Sgurr an Fhuarain if so desired. If a boat has been obtained on Loch Quoich, land at a point on the south shore opposite Gleann Cosaidh. From there the mountain can be climbed without difficulty.

From Sgurr Mor the main ridge is quite straightforward as far as An Eag, The 'Eag' or 'notch' being a curious joint-face which lies athwart the ridge a few yards east of the summit. From An Eag, the ridge to Sgurr nan Coireachan is very rocky and the ascent to the latter peak can be made to provide some scrambling. The mica-schist slabs of Coire nan Uth, on the south side of the ridge, are beautifully ice-moulded and are very smooth.

Sgurr nan Coireachan, 3125 ft. – To reach this mountain from

Upper Glendessarry take the Mam na Cloich' Airde track as far as the west bank of the Allt Coire nan Uth (see p. 70), and from there climb up the south shoulder of the hill. An alternative route of descent could either be by the stream running south from the Bealach nan Gall (the col immediately west of the mountain), or by the Coire nan Uth. If the latter route is taken in mist, avoid the steep slabs at the head of the corrie by descending the ridge leading to An Eag as far as the col (N.G.R. 938958). The lower part of the corrie is deeply-incised and is rather heavy going.

From the west end of the Loch Quoich Reservoir the ascent is best made by way of Druim Buidhe, up which a stalker's path can be followed for some distance.

Sgurr na Ciche, 3410 ft. – This well-known peak stands about $2\frac{1}{2}$ miles E.N.E. of the head of Loch Nevis. It is the highest in the district and from certain directions shows up as a beautiful cone-shaped mountain. Its eastern corrie, the Coire nan Gall, is very wild and rocky, but has no potential climbing. The mountain is very remote and since the enlargement of Loch Quoich, any route to the hill not using water transport involves a considerable amount of walking. In terms of total effort expended to reach the Sgurr, there is probably little to choose between the approaches from Glen Dessarry and Loch Quoich – at least in good weather. The usual round of Sgurr na Ciche and Sgurr nan Coireachan is not unduly arduous if taken from the north but is certainly easier from the Glen Dessarry side. In bad weather, with flooded streams, only the approach from the south should be used.

From Upper Glendessarry the best way of climbing the mountain (if Sgurr nan Coireachan is not to be included) is by way of the Bealach nan Gall (see above). From the Bealach follow the ridge over Garbh Chioch Bheag and Garbh Chioch Mhor, care being needed in hard winter conditions. Between the latter hill and Sgurr na Ciche drop down to a bealach – the Feadan na Ciche (*Feadan*, a whistle or chanter) thence climb up to the summit of the Sgurr. The ascent is slabby in places and near the top it is best to keep to the south side of the hill.

On the descent, an alternative route is to return to the Feadan and go down the gully leading south-west from it until one is below the steep crags which flank Garbh Chioch Mhor. A curious flat in the corrie, just below the rocks, can be traversed to a point overlooking the Mam na Cloich' Airde (point N.G.R. 904957). From there a long, easy descent to the south-east leads to the Mam track and thence to

Upper Glendessarry. Taken in reverse this is the easiest, if least inspiring, way to climb Sgurr na Ciche without making use of a boat.

From the north the ascent can be made by way of Coire nan Gall, which can be reached by rounding the cut-off dam at the west end of the Loch Quoich Reservoir. From the corrie a stalkers' path, shown on the one-inch map, strikes up the slopes of Meall a' Choire Dhuibh (2432 ft.). This path can be taken to the top of that hill and the north-east ridge of the Sgurr followed to the summit. The final rocks need care in winter. One can also ascend more directly from further up Coire nan Gall, over rock seamed with pegmatite veins.

The usual route of descent is by making the circuit of Coire nan Gall to Sgurr nan Coireachan and thence down the Druim Buidhe path.

The mountain can be climbed from the head of Loch Nevis and this is easiest way to reach the summit, but of course involves the hire of a boat. As the water at the head of the loch is very shallow even at high tide, land near Camusrory and reach the Mam na Cloich' Airde track by a long detour across the saltings at the mouth of the Carnoch River. Follow the Mam track to the head of the steep ascent from Loch Nevis and strike up into Coire na Ciche by a stalkers' path (not obvious) leading off to the left. One can then make for the south-west ridge, or for the Feadan, the former route being the easier and thence to the summit.

Druim a' Chuirn, 2680 ft. – While the full ridge from Sgurr Mor to Sgurr na Ciche forms the finest excursion in the area, it is a long and strenuous outing. A less demanding alternative is to start from Druim a' Chuirn, above Glendessary Lodge, and join the main ridge at An Eag. This is well worth doing if time presses. The ascent of Druim a' Chuirn from Glendessary Lodge is remarkably well-graded and easy. After the summit, the ridge becomes precipitous on the Kingie side but is quite straightforward to An Eag, at which point one has the choice of continuing either to Sgurr na Ciche or to Sgurr Mor. On the Feith a' Chichenais side of Druim a' Chuirn there are some very fine, rough slabs set at an easy angle. These can provide good, though discontinuous, scrambles.

Paths

Loch Arkaig to Tomdoun. – From Strathan a path, shown on the one-inch map, leads up the Dearg Allt to the bealach (*c.* 1500 ft.), between Fraoch Bheinn and Sgurr Mhurlagain, and thence follows the left bank of the Allt a' Chinn Bhric to Kinbreak, in Glen Kingie. No bridge exists at Kinbreak at the time of writing. Downstream, Glen Kingie is extremely boggy so the river should be crossed at once. (If the water is high it may be necessary to go more than a mile upstream before a crossing can be made. In spate it can be quite impracticable to cross for several miles upstream from Kinbreak and may not be possible at all downstream from it.) From the crossing near Kinbreak go up the hillside northwards for some distance and join the well-made path which leads north-east across the lower slopes of Sgurr an Fhuarain. Follow the path strictly, although it seems to climb needlessly high, to the Allt a' Choire Ghlais, from which it strikes due east to Lochan, $3\frac{1}{4}$ miles down the glen. From Lochan the path rises up, north-east round the east end of Gairich and from a junction, at a height of about 700 feet, strikes off almost due north past Lochan an Fhigheadair to the dam at the east end of Loch Quoich, 6 miles west from Tomdoun. There is no public right of way over the crest of the dam, but it is usually possible to cross the compensation outflow either below the dam or at several places downstream. Note that at the moment there is no direct access to Kingie through the new plantings at the end of the glen.

Branches of the above path are as follows:–

1. Reach Glen Kingie *via* Glendessary Lodge and the Feith a' Chicheanais. This route, while indirect, uses a lower pass than the Dearg Allt and brings one out higher up Glen Kingie where the crossing of a swollen stream is more likely to be practicable. Do not follow the path from the crest of the pass (*i.e.* point N.G.R. 975950) but head almost due north to the confluence of streams in Glen Kingie. Even at this point a crossing may not always be possible under high spate conditions.

2. At the Allt a' Choire Ghlais crossing a path to Loch Quoich side strikes off to the left. If arrangements have been made for a connecting boat, the loch can be crossed to the Kinloch Hourn road on the north side. There is no path on the south side and the going is terrible!

Loch Quoich to Carnoch, Loch Nevis. – See p. 80 for a description of this path, which provides the access route from Glen Garry to the Sgurr Mor-Sgurr na Ciche group.

Loch Arkaig to Loch Morar. – (1) *By Glen Pean.* – This route runs from the head of Loch Arkaig through Glen Pean to Oban at the east end of Loch Morar. The going is not nearly so good as that in the

Mam na Cloich' Airde (*q.v.*), but the summit level is only about 500 ft. Beyond Glen Pean Cottage (recently made habitable) the path (such as it is!) for a short distance is merely stepping-stones in the river and is liable to be covered in high spate. Continue on the north bank of the Pean and cross to the south bank at the ruins of an old bothy about ½ mile from the stepping-stones (difficult in spate). Loch Leum an t'Sagairt – in a most impressive situation – is passed by a path high up on its south bank. For the remainder of the way to Loch Morar the going is rough and the scenery very wild. From Oban one skirts round the east end of the loch to Kinlochmorar, from which a rough path leads along the north side of the loch to South Tarbet, four and a half miles from Kinlochmorar. There the track improves to Bracorina or one may cross over a low pass to Tarbet on Loch Nevis, to which a motor launch runs from Mallaig in summer. Check the service at Mallaig as it may be variable (see footnote p. 73). Private hire on Loch Morar can sometimes be arranged at Morar Hotel.

It is by no means unusual for the River Pean to become unfordable in spate conditions throughout its entire length from Loch Leum an t'Sagairt to Strathan. The loch *can* be passed by a laborious ascent on its north side but it is essential to climb well up the hillside to avoid sidestream gullies. This would, however, be preferable to following the south bank of the Pean all the way to (or from) Strathan, as some of the southern tributaries of the Pean are troublesome to cross under spate conditions.

(2) *By Gleann an Lochain Eanaiche.* – This route takes one to Kinlochmorar (ruin) at the head of the loch. From Upper Glendessarry slant downhill to cross the Dessarry by a bridge near A' Chuil (ruin), thence rough going along the south side of the river and up to the extraordinarily narrow bealach (*c.* 750 ft.) the head of Gleann an Lochain Eanaiche. A good track on the north side of the lochan leads down to Kinlochmorar. In good weather it is probably easier to take the Mam na Cloich' Airde track and ford the Dessarry near the confluence of the Allt Coire nan Uth.

This pass is bounded by slopes of remarkable steepness, that of Sgurr na h'Aide, above Lochain Eanaiche, being forty-five degrees for 2300 ft.

Loch Arkaig to Loch Nevis. This is the well-known pass of the Mam na Cloich' Airde. The path starts from Upper Glendessarry but is not obvious. Go uphill from the house for about 50 yards or so then traverse horizontally. The track rapidly improves and the going is quite straightforward to near the Allt Coire nan Uth, when the path once more becomes ill-defined. There is a bridge over the stream some distance downhill, but in good weather a generally horizontal line can be held and the burn easily crossed to rejoin the path ascending from the bridge. The route leads inwards through rock-scenery which steadily becomes more spectacular. The summit of the pass is about 1000 ft. above sea-level and is marked by a cairn. Some distance beyond, the remains of a tremendous landslip can be seen on the north side of the valley above two fair-sized lochans. After a sharp rise the path descends in a series of zig-zags to Sourlies (ruin) at the head of Loch Nevis.

The path ends at Sourlies, but as the loch there is shallow even at high tide, the nearest point to which a boat can normally be brought to pick up a party is Camusrory, a mile or so farther on. At low tide it is possible to follow the north shore of the loch (see O. S. map) until the saltings at the mouth of the Carnoch River can be traversed to Camusrory but normal high tide renders the route much more difficult and time-consuming. It may then be necessary to take to the steep hillside a few hundred yards beyond Sourlies to avoid an impasse, while the flooded saltings may force a long detour as far upstream as Carnoch. The probable state of the tides should be taken into account if arrangements have been made to meet a boat.

Boats from Mallaig call at Camusrory only by arrangement, but a path from Carnoch (see O.S. map) leads over the Mam Meadail and down to Inverie, where a service boat calls on certain days of the week (see p. 73).

7

Glen Garry and Knoydart

Gairich, 3105 ft. (026995)
Ben Aden, 2905 ft. (899986)
Meall Buidhe, 3107 ft. (849990)
Luinne Bheinn, 3083 ft. (869008)
Ladhar Bheinn, 3343 ft. (824040)
Sgurr a' Choire-Beithe, 2994 ft. (896015)
Sgurr nan Eugallt, 2934 ft. (931045)
Sgurr a' Mhaorach, 3365 ft. (984065)
Gleouraich, 3395 ft. (040054)
Spidean Mialach, 3268 ft. (066043)

Munro's Tables, section 7.

Maps: One-inch Ordnance Survey, 7th Series, Sheets 35 (mainly), 36. Half-inch Bartholomew latest edition, Sheet 50.

Glen Garry is one of Scotland's major glens, being 25 miles in length from the Great Glen to the watershed at the end of the Quoich Reservoir (Loch Quoich), and is continued in the same general line as a through-valley, past Lochan nam Breac, to Loch Nevis. The extraordinary assymmetry of the Western Highlands rivers is well exemplified here as from the col (*c.* 700 ft.), water flowing west reaches the sea at Loch Nevis in 6 miles while that flowing east does not reach the sea until Inverness, 60 miles away!

Glen Garry proper has two major lochs – Garry and Quoich. Correctly these should be referred to as the Garry and Quoich Reservoirs as they have been greatly enlarged from their natural state by impounding water by dams at the east end of the former Loch Garry and at *both* ends of the Quoich Reservoir. In times of low water the scar round their perimeters can be rather unsightly but under normal conditions is not sufficiently noticeable to detract from the view. In fact the writer quite categorically states that in his opinion the enlargement of the lochs has enhanced the overall scenery of the glen, especially around Loch Quoich. What it has done to the foot-access is quite another matter!

The eastern third of the glen is well wooded and, although most of this is planted conifer, enough natural woodland exists almost to nullify the usual sense of artificiality which this can give. This is either a happy chance or good planning and, if the latter, full marks to the planners!

At the eastern end of the glen Ben Tee rises finely out of the forest with a distinctly Scandinavian air about it but farther along Loch Garry the hills of the Arkaig–Garry watershed are too remote for their quite respectable northern corries to be appreciated fully. However this can be rectified by stopping at one or other of the lay-byes on the Garry–Moriston hill road where the prospect of Glen Garry, because of the increased height of the viewpoint, can truly be said to be absolutely magnificent. In the writer's opinion – and he is not alone – it is the finest mountain country prospect which can be had from any inland roadway in Scotland.

West from Tomdoun Hotel the scene becomes progressively more barren and wild until around Lochan nam Breac at the west end of Loch Quoich the scenery compares on equal terms with that of its three companion passes at the head of Loch Arkaig to the south. There is an immense amount of bare rock about, the country in large part corresponding to the area known to history and legend as the Rough Bounds. It certainly is rough! Even the road-bound tourist can sample it in the wild pass and steep descent to Kinloch Hourn.

It has been said that Loch Nevis and Loch Hourn rank second only to Loch Scavaig as the grandest of Scotland's sea-lochs and this is probably true.

Loch Hourn, especially, has an extremely narrow, steep walled upper reach (called Loch Beag), reminiscent of a Norwegian fiord, with which, in fact, it has geological affinities.

Although the hills of the Arkaig–Garry watershed could formerly be climbed from roads and tracks on the south side of Lochs Garry and Poulary, long walks were involved over country which is now growing forest. As a result the recommended routes to these hills are from Loch Arkaig side and anyone wishing to climb them from Glen Garry should make inquiries locally about the present state of the tracks shown on the 7th Series Ordnance map. The Forestry Office is a mile or so beyond Invergarry, on the north side of the River Garry. It was on one of these tracks, beside the Allt Garaidh Ghualaich that the writer encountered an otter, about a mile from the loch and heading strongly for the hills!

Most mountaineers will not worry unduly about relative inaccessibility of these hills. Instead, they will head for the more interesting mountains around Loch Quoich or arrange, with some careful logistics, a foray into the mountainous peninsula of Knoydart.

Many of the hills can be reached from the road along Loch Garry and Loch Quoich to Kinloch Hourn. (Make sure you have a recent map as there has been much re-alignment of the roads herabouts because of the loch enlargement), but the hills round the head of Loch Quoich are pretty inaccessible and most are more easily taken from the Loch Arkaig side. However, if one can face the long and in part trackless walks, there is no doubt that aesthetically this is the side from which to approach them. Camping of course helps, but is specifically forbidden beside the road from Kingie to the pass above Kinloch Hourn.

Peninsular Knoydart – that is the part to the west of the Carnoch River and Barrisdale Bay – has not of recent years proved very receptive to casual climbers. At the time of writing the estate has recently changed hands and, for those who wish to arrange access, the estate office is at Inverie, by Mallaig.

The Knoydart hills can be reached by boat from Mallaig, either by service boat on certain days calling at Inverie and Tarbet, or to various parts by private hire. Check times and availability at Mallaig.* Alternatively, Arnisdale is a possible centre, but this definitely involves boat hire which can only be arranged by private treaty with local folk and so involves a visit. For the hardy, foot access from the east is possible to the major hills (see below).

The area has perhaps less historical interest than those already discussed, but this may be due to the author's ignorance! Invergarry Castle – an old stronghold of the MacDonnells – lies on Loch Oich side. It was blown up by Cumberland after Culloden but the shell remains. It can be visited by application to Glengarry Castle Hotel, on whose ground it lies.

Prince Charlie, during his days in the heather, must have had a trying time around the Kinloch Hourn road watershed. A line of sentries had been established to head him off from eastern Scotland but he broke through the cordon, almost within talking distance of the soldiers, somewhere about Coire Shubh, from where he made his way into Glenmoriston.

It was not, however, the first visit of English forces to the district.

* At the time of writing the services are operated by Bruce Watt Cruises.

General Monk, Cromwell's hatchet man in Scotland, is reputed to have led his forces into the Loch Loyne area during his pacification operations following the Montrose uprising. No doubt he carried out the operation with the professional competence which seems to be the hall-mark of this remarkable soldier, who amongst his other achievements, built the first fort at what became Fort William, and later became Admiral of the Fleet.

The Glen Garry–Loch Hourn through valley, like so many others in the Western Highlands, was an old drove-route for cattle coming from the Isles to the southern markets and the path from Kinloch Hourn to Arnisdale by the Dubh Lochans follows the line of the drove-road. In more modern times it is a testing section of the Scottish Six-Day Motor Cycle Trial. It seems impossible! If following the track by Kinloch Hourn House a stand of Blue Gum (Eucalyptus) trees provides an exotic sight but as yet there are no wallabies to be found, being so far only reported in Britain in Yorkshire.

Gairich, 3015 ft. – This is the finely shaped mountain which stands on the south side of the east end of Loch Quoich, and is such a prominent and beautiful feature in the view looking up Glen Garry. The hill is mostly grassy, although there are some steepish rocks on the north-east face. It is most conveniently ascended from the Quoich Dam. The footwalk over the crest of the dam is not open to the public, but it is normally possible to cross the restricted outflow from the loch either immediately below the dam or at several places downstream. A short distance westwards from the dam, on the south side of the reservoir, a good path leads south across the hills to Lochan in Glen Kingie. This path should be followed for about 1¾ miles to where it is joined by a rough cart-road coming up from Loch Quoich. From this point a stalkers' path leads up the long east shoulders of Gairich to a height of about 1600 feet. From the end of this path follow the rounded shoulder of the hill, with fine views to the right into the north-east corrie, to the foot of the final peak. The climb up the latter is steep and in places narrow, and it affords a little mild climbing if the actual edge is rigidly adhered to; but otherwise it is quite easy. The summit is rather flat, has two cairns, and commands a magnificent view to the west. If an alternative descent is considered note that the reservoir now covers the track on the south side of the former Loch Quoich. This track is shown on early 7th Series maps. The going is now terrible!

Ben Aden 2905 ft. – Ben Aden is now seldom climbed as most folk approaching from Loch Quoich head straight for Sgurr na Ciche, Nonetheless it is a good viewpoint, which should be included if possible.

The best way to climb it is to come from Loch Nevis and combine its ascent with that of Sgurr na Ciche. There is no difficulty in following the ridge round over Meall a' Choire Duibh but the ascent to the Sgurr is steep, needing care in snow conditions. If you are coming from Loch Quoich side, follow the Loch Quoich–Loch Nevis route described on page 80 as far as the cut-off dam near Lochan na Cruadach. Then go over Meall a'Choire Duibh by the path from Coire nan Gall shown on the one-inch map.

There is an immense amount of granite pegmatite hereabouts.

Sgurr na Ciche. For Sgurr na Ciche see Chapter 6.

Meall Buidhe, 3107 ft. **Luinne Bheinn,** 3083 ft. – These are the culminating points of the group of mountains which extends from the upper reach of Loch Nevis to Glen Barrisdale. They are wild and craggy in character, and the great corrie on the north-west side of the ridge, which connects the two hills, is a good example of glaciated rock. The summit of Meall Buidhe consists of a broad ridge running east and west, with two tops of nearly equal height. The west top is the higher and is mossy. The east top is smaller, is of a bolder character, and on its northern side there is a fine precipice, the Creag Dhearg.

From the east top a steep ridge drops down E.N.E. towards the long, narrow, and hummocky ridge which leads to Luinne Bheinn. There is also a broad and not very steep ridge running out E.S.E. to Sgurr Sgeithe. These two ridges enclose the eastern corrie of the mountain, which is one of its finest features.

Luinne Bheinn has fewer features of interest, and it consists of a fairly narrow ridge, running generally from east to west, with steep slopes on either side.

The combined ascent of the two hills is a pleasant day's outing. It can be done from Inverie by way of Gleann Meadail, to the ford and thence up to the west ridge of Meall Buidhe which is followed to the summit. From the east top descend steeply to 'Bealach' (Ile Coire) and thence over Druim Leac a 'Shith to the foot of the steep ascent to Luinne Bheinn. This mountain can be descended by way of the north-west ridge to the Mam Barrisdale path for the return to Inverie. An alternative circuit is from Carnoch, at the head of Loch Nevis, by the Mam Meadail path for the ascent and Gleann Unndalain for the descent to the Carnoch River.

Luinne Bheinn may also be climbed from the Kinloch Hourn road. Leave the car near the bridge over the Caolie Water thence follow the route for Ben Aden, etc., given under 'Paths' below (p. 80). It is best to cross to the south side of the pass at the cut-off dam, although this may seem a needless diversion, and follow the path on that side as far as the east end of Lochan nam Breac. Stepping-stones here are often under water. Now cross to the north side and follow the path on the north side of the Lochan. In a short time the path begins to climb up the hillside, and ultimately crosses the east shoulder of Luinne Bheinn at a height of about 2050 ft., from which point an easy and gradual ascent leads to the summit.

Ladhar Bheinn, 3343 ft. – This grand mountain (whose name is phonetically rendered as 'Larven') stands on the south of Loch Hourn to the west of Barrisdale Bay. It consists of a high summit ridge, about two miles in length, running from north-west to south-east. The south-west slope is grassy and uninteresting. The north-east face contains a number of corries and is the finest feature of the mountain. Coire Dhorrcail, especially, is deep, with rather impressive cliffs round its headwall which have attracted the attention of climbers from time to time. The ridges bounding the corries are narrow, especially that north east of the summit on which lies the subsidiary top of Stob a'Choire Odhair (3138 ft.). At the south east end of the main ridge Aonach Sgoilte (the 'split' is an obvious gully on the south side) forms a curious T-shaped termination. The buttress on the north-east end of the cross-bar is best circumvented by descending to the south-east before the end of the ridge is reached.

From Inverie the ascent of the mountain is perfectly simple. Follow the path from the village through the Mam Uidhe into Gleann na Guiserein, and then strike eastwards up that glen to Folach, and climb up the south slope of the mountain to the summit. The return of course should be made over Aonach Sgoilte.

The most interesting way to climb the mountain is from Barrisdale Bay (or Inbhir Dhorrcail), which may be reached from Arnisdale, if suitable arrangements have been made for a boat. From Barrisdale Bay, the easiest route is probably to make for the entrance to Coire Dhorrcail by a path on the east side of the stream issuing from that corrie. When the corrie is reached make for the Bealach Coire Dhorrcail on the main ridge, and follow the latter to the summit. The descent should be made by the north-east ridge to Stob a' Choire Odhair, and down to Loch Hourn.

The mountain has been ascended by this route with the variation that Barrisdale Bay was reached by walking from Kinloch Hourn along the path on the south side of the loch. This made a long, strenuous, but magnificent day's outing.

It is possible, with nautical cunning, for dinghy-borne climbers to ease the Loch Hournside journey by careful choice of tides. Leaving on the turn from Kinloch Hourn, the ebb helps greatly on the outward run leaving just enough time on the hill for a return on the flood. If one gets delayed however, the strong currents in the narrows test the powers of a small outboard engine! It might just be possible by canoe, and certainly the canoe trip to Barrisdale on the tides is a magnificent journey in the summer with all manner of sea-birds and probably several seals to liven the trip. Loch Beag – the eastern enclosed part of Loch Hourn – dries out for a longish distance at low tide, as does Barrisdale Bay.

The cliffs of Coire Dhorrcail have attracted climbers over the years. The cirque of crags there attains a height of 1200 ft. while in the subsidiary Coire na Cabaig to the east of the main corrie there is another steep precipice of 700–800 ft. Despite their promising appearance these crags have not yielded any good summer climbs, the rock being slabby micaceous granulite, mossy and of adverse lie. First class winter routes have been recorded (see Rock Climbs section) but this was in an exceptionally hard season (1962) and since then it is doubtful if there have been comparable conditions, at least for any length of time. Good snow for climbing is rarely found on these hills near the western seaboard.

Sgurr a' Choire-bheithe, 2994 ft. – This is the western end and highest top of the long Druim Chosaidh which runs west from the head of Loch Quoich for about five miles to Glen Barrisdale, the eastern summit being Sgurr Airidh na Beinne (2538 ft.). Taken from east to west, the traverse of the mountain gives a very interesting walk. The ridge is pretty rugged, but provides no climbing. The views on either side are magnificent. For the descent, one should drop down to the Barrisdale path in the bealach, the Mam Unndalain, between Sgurr a' Choire-bheithe and Luinne Bheinn, and then return to Loch Quoich through the Lochan nam Breac pass (see p. 80).

Sgurr nan Eugallt, 2933 ft. – This is the culminating point of the rather rugged set of hills which extends from Loch Quoich to the head of Loch Hourn, a distance of fully 5 miles. The range has four distinct summits, all shown on the one-inch map.

The whole ridge is a pleasant walk, but most people will be content with Sgurr nan Eugallt and Sgurr Sgiath Airidh (2890 ft. *pron.* 'Skiary'). These mountains are certainly worth climbing and can be approached easily by means of good stalker's path from Coireshubh on the Kinloch Hourn road. An Caisteal (*c.* 2130 ft.) two miles west from Sgurr Sgiath Airidh is slabby, circular and has one recorded rock-climb.

Sgurr a'Mhaoraich, 3365 ft. – This mountain stands at the head of Loch Beag at the extreme eastern end of Loch Hourn and on the north side of Loch Quoich. Looking up the former, it appears to block all exit from the valley, the steep road-pass being invisible on the right.

Sgurr a Mhaoraich itself is the culmination of a pretty extensive group of ridges and lower summits between Loch Quoich and Wester Glen Quoich, of which Am Bathaich about three-quarters of a mile to the north, is *c.* 3055 ft. high.

One can select various traverses of the mountain according to one's own wishes, by way of the numerous paths shown on the one-inch map. Probably the best circuit is to start with that which commences at N.G.R. 995035 (approximately) near a footbridge over the Caolie Water, soon after the road leaves Loch Quoich to pass over to Kinloch Hourn. From the summit the mountaineer has a really stupendous view down the long, narrow, rugged trench of Loch Hourn. The descent can be made over Am Bathaich and the zig-zag path to Alltbeithe, in Western Glen Quoich.

Gleouraich, 3395 ft. **Spidean Mialach,** 3268 ft. – These two mountains stand on the north side of the eastern end of Loch Quoich, their summits being the culminating points of a long ridge, about two miles in length, which runs parallel to Loch Quoich. Gleouriach stands at the west end of the ridge, and overlooks the lower part of Glen Quoich. Half a mile east from the summit is the east top of Gleouraich (3291 ft.), beyond which the main ridge drops down steeply to the Fiar Bealach (2433 ft.), and then rises up to the peak of Spidean Mialach, which is $1\frac{1}{4}$ miles south-east from the east top of Gleouraich.

Like most of the hills in the district, the south slopes are mostly grassy with screes on the higher parts. The north slopes are much steeper and contain rocky corries which hold snow well on into late spring. The finest parts of the north face are the Garbh Choire Mor and the Garbh Choire Beag, which lie north of the ridge between the two tops of Gleouraich; but it is doubtful if any good rock climbing could be found in them.

All the tops of the group can be climbed in an easy day from the shore of Loch Quoich. Spidean Mialach is most quickly climbed from the road about ½ mile or so east of the Loch Quoich Dam, from which it is only 1¼ miles distant, but it is better to drive to the bridge over the Allt a' Mheil and walk up the good stalkers' path (not on the map) which starts from the roadside immediately to the east of the bridge. The Allt a' Mheil glen should be followed for about 1¼ miles, and the final slopes of the Spidean then taken to. Going westwards along the main ridge there is a rather big drop to the Fiar Bealach, and then a fairly steep rocky ascent, with a stalkers' path, up to the east top of Gleouraich. The walk between Gleouraich and Spidean takes about one hour. From Gleouraich the best descent is to follow the ridge westwards for half a mile, and then follow it southwards by a good stalkers' path which goes right down to the high road just west of the bridge over the Allt Coire Peitireach, ¾ of a mile west from the car.

Mullach Coire Ardachaidh, 1760 ft. – This is a very minor hill round which curves the new Invergarry–Glenmoriston road. Its claim to inclusion in this Guide is the excellent view from its summit, which may easy be attained from the road. Under good snow conditions its slopes provide some fair skiing.

Paths

Formerly a plexus of excellent paths radiated from the shooting lodge of Kinlochquoich at the head of the natural Loch Quoich, but these are now truncated by the enlarged loch and terminate on the loch side. No connecting links between them have been established. All the paths are shown on the one-inch map and their utility is best left to the individual climber to assess with reference to his own particular purpose. Note in particular however, that none of the major side-streams entering the loch is bridged and as some can prove very difficult to cross under spate conditions, access to the paths can be awkward at times.

The former Kinlochquoich–Loch Nevis path was the main route to many of the hills described in Chapter 7 and was an alternative

79

approach to some in Chapter 6; as the track is now inundated the route which replaces it merits detailed description:

Loch Quoich to Carnoch, Loch Nevis: Leave the Tomdoun-Kinloch Hourn road where it leaves Loch Quoich to pass over to Kinloch Hourn. Cross the bridge and contour well above the shores of the loch (when water is high, the reservoir extends almost up to the bridge) until the remains of the former Kinlochquoich road can be joined after about 1½ miles. Follow the road westwards until it dips into the loch, then continue along the trackless hillside to Gleann Cosaidh. The Amhainn Chosaidh is very difficult to cross in spate and may merit the use of a safety rope. (In times of high flood it can be impassable for miles upstream.) A few hundred yards westwards from the stream the remains of a construction road lead from the loch shore and can be followed to the cut-off dam near Lochan na Cruadhach. At the dam, cross to the south side of the valley and join the original path through the pass. At the east end of Lochan nam Breac cross to the north side of the valley by some rather ineffective stepping-stones, whence the path continues above the north side of the loch. (It is possible to follow a poor track direct from the north side of the cut-off dam to Lochan nam Breac.) Near the west end of the loch the path, after a biggish rise, drops into a desolate hollow containing ruins. Just beyond this hollow, a path leading to Barrisdale (see below) strikes up steeply to the right by short zig-zags and, from the foot of them, the Carnoch path diverges, on the level, to the left. It is not shown on the one-inch map and leads into the ravine of the river, through some woods. Near its exit from these the track is rather ill-defined and may be difficult to spot if approach is made from Carnoch. Carnoch itself is now a ruin, the present shooting lodge being at Camusrory, some distance beyond. Boats from Mallaig call at Camusrory by prior arrangement only.

The natural walking continuation of this route is by a path (see O.S. map) from Carnoch over the Mam Meadail to Inverie where a post-boat from Mallaig calls several times each week in summer. There is a telephone at Inverie by which the boat-hirers at Mallaig can be contracted if necessary prior arrangements have been made.

Branch paths to Barrisdale, Loch Hourn: There are two routes both shown on the one-inch map. Of these, the one over the Mam Unndalain (the only path shown on the map west of Lochan nam Breac) is very pleasant. The other by way of Gleann Cosaidh is

18. The Road to the Isles. Loch Eilt.

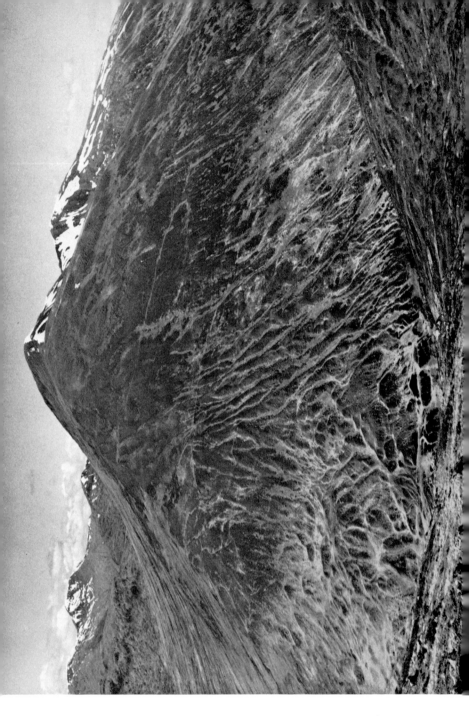

19. Culvain. Dead winter grass forms a pattern in the stream runnels. Sgurr Mor (Kingie) behind.

20. Beinn Bhan and Glen Loy. The smooth hills of the eastern part of Lochaber.

21. Streap Comhlaidh and Streap from Sgurr Thuilm. Ben Nevis and the Grampians beyond.

22. Glenfinnan. Beinn Gharbh on the left, Sgurr Thuilm on the right.

rather dreary in the Gleann Cosaidh section. It passes by Loch an Lagain Aintheich, in a curious hollow set right athwart the watershed, over which in late Glacial times Loch Quoich probably spilled. From there down Glen Barrisdale the scenery is much more attractive.

8

Glen Moriston, Glen Shiel and Glenelg

Carn Ghluasaid, 3140 ft. (146124)
Sgurr nan Conbhairean, 3635 ft. (130139)
Tigh Mor, 3285 ft. (133154)
A'Chralaig, 3673 ft. (094148)
Mullach Fraoch-choire, 3614 ft. (095170)
Creag a'Mhaim, 3102 ft. (088077)
Druim Shionnach, 3222 ft. (074084)
Aonach air Chrith, 3342 ft. (051082)
Maol Chinn-dearg, 3214 ft. (032087)
Sgurr an Doire Leathain, 3272 ft. (015097)
Sgurr an Lochain, 3282 ft. (005104)
Creag nan Damh, 3012 ft. (982112)
The Saddle, 3314 ft. (935130)
Sgurr na Sgine, 3098 ft. (945114)
Beinn Sgritheall, 3196 ft. (836127)
Mealfuarvonie, 2284 ft. (458223)

Munro's Tables, Sections 7 and 8.

Maps: One-inch Ordnance Survey 7th Series, Sheets 35 and 36. Half-inch Bartholomew latest edition, Sheet 50.

The Glen Moriston–Glen Shiel through valley is the major east-west pass across the Western Highlands and has long been the trade route from Skye to the Great Glen. This is because the main watershed of the area lies well back from the long inlet of Loch Duich, allowing a more gentle ascent for track or road than is the case for the steep headwalls of the western valleys to the south.

Followed from the Great Glen, the floor of the valley is at first quite narrow, but becomes wider after five miles or so to form a broad strath until Loch Cluanie is reached. This section is devoid of mountaineering interest and Mealfuarvonie (2284 ft.) is only included in this section because of lack of anywhere else to put it. It properly belongs to the Great Glen and its only claim to fame is that it is the highest mountain in Scotland which is made out of Old Red Sandstone.

At Loch Cluanie, however, things change dramatically as the road enters the mountainous area to the west. The hills of Ceannacroc

Forest to the north of the loch only serve as an introduction to the magnificent mountain scenery of Strath (or Glen) Cluanie and Glen Shiel to the west. Indeed Glen Shiel must have an equal claim with Glencoe and Glen Torridon as one of the finest road passes in Britain.

The numerous high mountains in the area render logical description difficult as there are too many for one chapter based on a valley-to-valley division. The precedent of the previous Guide has therefore been followed in separating the Kintail district north of Glen Shiel for separate treatment. The present chapter will deal with the Ceanna-croc Forest (on the north side of the through valley) and with the south side of the valley including also the Glenelg area beyond the Bealach Ratagain.

Because of its character as a thoroughfare the valley and its neighbourhood has a long strategic history. Probably the oldest evidence for this are the remarkably well preserved Iron Age 'Brochs' or Pictish Towers of Gleann Beag, near Glenelg. These are the best examples of such structures to be found on the Scottish Mainland and one of them is second only to that of Mousa in the Shetlands in respect of preservation. They seem to have been purely defensive, possibly against coastal slave-raiders.

The next military structure was probably Eilean Donan Castle (mentioned in the next chapter) and James I of Scotland may have made a foray up Glen Moriston in pursuit of Alasdair of the Isles following a battle somewhere near Fort Augustus (which he reached, incidentally, by crossing the Corrieyairack Pass).

James left no trace, however, and the next evidence of warlike occupation is the Barracks of Bernera at Glenelg. At them the military road leading from Wade's Great Glen road to Kylerhea for Skye, terminated after an arduous ascent over the Bealach (or Mam) Ratagain from Kintail. This old road, whose traces are wrongly named 'General Wade's Road' on some maps, was in fact constructed by one of his successors. In 1773 Dr. Johnson and James Boswell traversed the completed portion and the heavy Doctor had to ride two horses alternately on the way down from the Bealach Ratagain section. Cattle used to be swum across Kyle Rhea at slack water, in groups of several animals tied tail-under-next-chin, *en route* from Skye to the southern markets.

The 'Battle of Glen Shiel' commemorated by a sign half-way down the glen near the new bridge, is the site of a curious and little-known

83

incident when a small Jacobite force with a token supporting group of 300 or so Spanish soldiery landed to attempt a rising on behalf of the Old Pretender (James III) in 1719. They surrendered after a somewhat confused skirmish in which, according to the 'Statistical Account of 1845', no less a person than the celebrated Rob Roy MacGregor took part! If this is true then he was far from his home Braes of Balquhidder and at any rate he seems to have done more harm than good to the Highland cause. The encounter is remembered in the name of the mountain above, Sgurr nan Spainteach – the Spaniard's Peak.

Prince Charles Edward, after breaking through the cordon at Coire Shubh (see Chapter 7) reached Glen Shiel near Achnangart. After nearly climbing Sgurr nan Conbhairean (and spending a night out there) he spent a week with the 'Seven Men of Glenmoriston', who had fought for him at Culloden, in Prince Charlie's Cave in the headwaters of the River Doe, near Ceannacroc. On leaving, he crossed the hills to Glen Affric.

The Ceannacroc Forest

On the north side of the Glen Moriston–Glen Shiel through valley the mountains form two distinct groups east and west of An Caorunn Mor, a deep glen which runs from Strath Cluanie to Alltbeithe in Glen Affric. To the west lie the mountains of Kintail, to the east the Ceannacroc Forest comprises a large group of high mountains lying on the north side of Loch Cluanie and extending northwards into Glen Affric for a distance of about seven miles. The massif decreases in height east of the River Doe and the Allt Garbh, but in all is one of the largest defined mountain groups in the Highlands, comprising five 'Munros' and eight 'tops'. The southern slopes of the hills are smooth and rounded, Carn Ghluasaid especially looking rather like a 'Cairngorm' from the Garry–Moriston hill road. The east and north sides are steeper, with some deep corries, while those north of the summit of Sgurr nan Conbhairean on its east side are very rocky. No good rock-climbing routes can be seen however, but there is a good chance of some pretty testing snow-and-rock routes. The area would be well worth exploring in winter, but is very inaccessible.

Sgurr nan Conbhairean, 3635 ft. **Carn Ghluasaid,** 3140 ft. etc. – These hills can very easily be climbed from Lundie on the new Glen Moriston road. A path following the line of the old military road leads off the main road near a small memorial to the victim of an exposure accident on these hills in January 1960, and, in about half a mile, a hill path diverges on the north [N.G.R. 137103]. This leads to the summit of Carn Ghluasaid (3140 ft.) from which a broad ridge leads in a general north-west direction to Sgurr nan Conbhairean by way of the 3260 ft. 'top' of Creag a' Chaoruinn and the Glas Bealach. It is perhaps worth noting that the smooth, easy slopes from here to the summit of Sgurr nan Conbhairean can become wind-swept and icy even when deep powder snow lies at lower levels. The writer found progress impossible without crampons at Easter 1970. At the same time a large avalanche had fallen quite close to the path on the way up to Carn Ghluasaid. The ridge W.S.W. from Sgurr nan Conbhairean can become pleasantly narrow in snow conditions but leads easily round the corrie of the little Gorm Lochan by way of Drochaid an Tuill Easaich (*c*. 3300 ft.) from which an easy descent can be made to Meall Breac and the old Military Road. It is better to return by this to the car rather than to trust to the avoiding skill of the drivers on the Cluanie-side race track.

The ridge north from Sgurr nan Conbhairean to Tigh Mor (3285 ft.) is a long and quite pleasant walk. It can be extended over Tigh Mor na Seilge (3045 ft.) but as one will have to retrace one's steps, most folk will be content with the main top.

Near the 3285 ft. top of the one-inch map the author in 1969 found the remains of an *al fresco* lunch of about 1890. An old Schweppes bottle (cork type) of that period was discovered stuck in wasting peat where some one-time tidy soul had buried it. Perhaps it serves as a warning to modern litter-depositing parties (or a fine example to glass bottle makers ?).

A genuine Prince Charlie's Cave is marked on the map below Tigh Mor na Seilge in Coire Mheadhoin, whose burn is one the headwaters of the River Doe. It is not really a cave but a kind of Shelter Stone formed from several large boulders. The Prince stayed there for a week with the seven Glenmoriston men.

A'Chralaig, 3673 ft. **Mullach Fraoch-choire,** 3614 ft. This ridge of mountains lies west of An Caorunn Mor and is separated from the Sgurr nan Conbhairean group by the Bealach Coir' a' Chait (2381 ft.). The ridge runs almost north-south for about five miles and can be reached easily from the main road. The initial slopes first rise up to an unnamed top from which a spur ridge leads north east for about a mile to A'Chioch (*c*. 3050 ft. – the O.S. name seems to have been applied to the end of the spur much farther on). From the unnamed top, however, the main ridge rises about half-a-mile to the summit of A'Chralaig (3673 ft. – the pronunciation rhymes with 'chrawley'). From there to Mullach Fraoch-choire the ridge runs almost due north, a distance of about 1½ miles, with some pinnacles, easily turned on the west side. The Mullach has three tops. The south top (3295 ft.) is shown on the map, the main top (3614 ft.) is the main summit and the north-east top (3435 ft.) lies about ½ mile farther on but is not shown on the map.

The South Side of Glen Shiel

Aonach air Chrith, 3342 ft. **Sgurr an Lochain,** 3282 ft. etc. – On the south side of Strath Cluanie and at the eastern end of Glen Shiel lies one of the longest groups of mountains in Scotland. Even excluding an extension to Sgurr a'Bhac Chaolais to the west, for which a logical claim for inclusion might be entered, the 'South Glen Shiel Ridge' measures nearly 7 miles in a straight line, from Creag a'Mhaim in the east to Creag nan Damh in the west. On it lie seven separate summits over 3000 ft. in height (all Munros), and for a length of six miles it never falls below a height of 2500 ft. The southern slopes of the hills, although exhaustingly steep, are mostly grassy. The northern side has some quite respectable corries which although rocky in some cases, have not much summer climbing potential.

Under good snow conditions the traverse of the ridge is without doubt one of the finest high-level walks in Scotland, being nowhere difficult under normal conditions, although quite narrow in places. In summer it is a pleasant scamper for those in good training.

In order to climb the South Glen Shiel Ridge in its entirety the point of access is, at the eastern end, the locked gate on the old Cluanie–Tomdoun road, a few yards from the Cluanie Lodge road junction. Creag a'Mhaim can be climbed without difficulty from the bridge over the Allt Giubhais about a mile beyond the locked gate or, even more easily, by a much longer route to the summit of the road and the path shown on the map on the east-south-east terminal ridge of the mountain. This path actually goes almost to the top instead of stopping a short distance up as the map shows. The western point of access is the path from Mhalagain Bridge near Achnangart, to Bealach Duibh Leac, west of Creag nan Damh.

There is no difficulty on any part of the ridge which comprises, from west to east, Creag nan Damh 3012 ft. – followed to the east by the lowest bealach on the ridge at 2383 ft.), Sgurr Beag (2926 ft.), Sgurr an Lochain (3282 ft.), Sgurr an Doire Leathain (3272 ft. – the actual summit is about 180 yds. north of the main ridge), Sgurr Coire na Feinne (2958 ft.), Maol Chinn-dearg (3214 ft.), Aonach Air Chrith (3342 ft.), Druim Shionnach (3222 ft. – flat topped and rounded and not named on the one-inch map) and Creag a'Mhaim (3102 ft.). This traverse takes about 9 hours for a moderate party including time to admire the view and is best done with two cars.

A shorter day can be had with one car only by parking near the watershed on the road about 2½ miles west from Cluanie Inn (a small river tunnel permits crossing here) and climbing Sgurr an Lochain past the little corrie loch. The ridge can be traversed eastwards as far as desired and a return made to the road by any of the northerly spurs. All these are easy except that north from the summit of Aonach air Chrith which is rocky and can be difficult in winter. In summer the difficulties can be by-passed. New forestry works near the road do not as yet interfere much with access.

The narrowest part of the ridge is from Maol Chinn-dearg to Aonach air Chrith and has some cliffs on its north side. Coir' an t-Slugain has fine cliffs in its headwall, with one recorded rock-climb and some snow gullies in season. On the west side of A'Chioch, a shapely peak at the end of the ridge N.N.E. of the summit on Aonach air Chrith, are some steep rocks with one snow gully.

The ridge can be reached from Alltbeithe in Glen Quoich by one or other of several unmapped paths which zig-zag up the south slopes of the hills. It is an unattractive way.

The Saddle, 3314 ft. – This mountain, with Sgurr an Sgine and Faochag really forms a continuation of the South Glen Shiel chain west of the Bealach Duibh Leac and a rather negligible summit called Sgurr a' Bhac Chaolais. A deep bealach, however, separates them from the more continuous high level ridge, and they are best made into a day's trip on their own.

The Saddle (whose height was formerly given as 3317 ft. on the Popular Edition map) is without doubt the most interesting hill in the whole of the Glen Shiel and Kintail area. It is precipitous, with rocky corries and narrow and in places pinnacled, ridges. The actual summit of the mountain consists of a narrow ridge about 1½ miles in length, running almost due west and east from Spidean Dhomhuill Bhric (3082 ft.) to Sgurr na Forcan (c. 3100 ft.), and continuing beyond the latter for some distance.

From a short distance below the summit of the Saddle a transverse ridge runs out northwards for about ½ mile, terminating at Sgurr na Creige, where a golden eagle has been known to nest. Hence the local name Sgurr Nid na h-Iolaire (The Peak of the Eagle's Nest).

At Spidean Dhomhuill Bhric the main ridge turns north, broadens out, and, passing over the uninteresting summit of Sgurr Leac nan Each (3013 ft.), becomes hummocky, and may be said to terminate at Sgurr a' Gharg Gharaidh (2252 ft.).

The south slopes of the Saddle are mostly steep and rocky, except where easy grassy slopes abut on the main ridge to the west of the summit. North of the main ridge there are two fine corries, separated by the Sgurr na Creige ridge, Coir' Uaine to the west, and Coire Caol to the east. The former is the finer, and the precipitous north-west face of the Saddle overlooking it is cleaved by a great gully, which was first climbed at Easter 1926. The most convenient routes of ascent of the Saddle are:

From Invershiel. – There is a good path (shown on the one-inch map) up the Allt Undalain which should be followed until the stream forks from which point the north end of Sgurr na Creige is climbed, and the north ridge followed to the summit of the Saddle. The route is rocky and in places high up is narrow, but is nowhere difficult.

From Glen Shiel. – The shortest route to the summit is from Mhalagain Bridge, near Achnangart, in Glen Shiel. The path leads up the west slope of the glen to the top of the ridge between Glen Shiel and Coire Caol, and it is then a simple matter to reach the foot of the Sgurr na Forcan ridge. The climb up the latter, and, from it, along the exceedingly narrow summit ridge of the Saddle to the highest point, is certainly the most sporting route to the summit, and presents no difficulties to experienced climbers. It is not recommended for those who are hill-walkers only.

In winter the climb up the rocky section of this ridge to the summit of Sgurr na Forcan and the traverse of the col between it and the main top is a mountaineering route which may be at least Grade II in standard. It is well worth doing, but is only for the experienced.

From Kinloch Hourn. – Quite an interesting and easy way to the Saddle is from Kinloch Hourn by way of the path, shown on the one-inch map, to the Bealach a'Chasain and thence up over Spidean Domhuill Bhric. The track is part of an old drove road from Kyle Rhea to the Great Glen.

Some fair rock climbing can be had on the south face of the Forcan

23. Stob a'Ghrianain, Coire Dubh.

24. Loch Arkaig, looking west. The shoulder of Culvain (on extreme left), Streaps, Sgurr Thuilm, Glen Pean (at head of loch).

25. The Streaps and Sgurr Thuilm from above Glendessarry Lodge.

26. Sgurr na Ciche.

27. Sgurr na h-Aide, Gleann an Lochain Eainache and the Mam na Cloich'Airde.

28. Glen Garry. Loch Poulary and the Glen Kingie hills.

29. Ben Tee and Meall a'Choire Ghlais from Glen Garry, near Greenfield.

30. Gairich.

31. Loch Quoich. Rising from the loch, on left, Sgurr an Fhuarain, Sgurr Mor. The Garbh Chiochs and Sgurr na Ciche at the head of the loch with Ben Aden on right. Sgurr a'Choire-bheithe extreme right. (The loch now covers the islands on left).

32. Gleouraich and Spidean Mialach. Late evening on the Loch Quoich reservoir.

33. Loch Hourn and Ladhar Bheinn from Sgurr a'Mhaoraich.

34. Lochan nam Breac. Sgurr Mor behind.

Ridge above Bealach Coire Mhalagain (see Rock Climbs, Appendix II).

Sgurr na Sgine, 3098 ft. **Faochag,** *c.* 3010 ft. – These mountains form a horseshoe with the Saddle, from which they are separated by the Bealach Coire Mhalagain (2291 ft.). The Bealach can be reached from the Saddle by dropping down grassy slopes from the west top and traversing across as soon as easy ground is gained but it would be a pity to miss out the Forcan Ridge if one has not already come up that way. From the foot of the ridge the Bealach can be gained by traversing below the cliffs and this is probably the easiest way from Glen Shiel even if one is not climbing the Saddle.

Sgurr na Sgine can be climbed without trouble from the Bealach, but in mist note that there is a rather deceptive top north from the real summit. Then back-track to Faochag and descend by way of its steep nose north-east to Mhalagain Bridge.

It was probably Faochag that Dr. Johnson claimed was not, as Boswell had it, 'an immense mountain', but only a 'considerable protuberance'! From Glen Shiel it shows up as a splendid cone.

Beinn Sgritheall, 3196 ft. – This fine mountain, whose long-accustomed name of Bein Sgriol has been somewhat dramatically, if no doubt correctly, altered on the 7th Series map, lies on the north side of Loch Hourn and shows up well in views from the Sound of Sleat, grassy and tree-clad below with great smooth scree slopes above. On the north there are two huge sterile corries divided by the north-east shoulder of the mountain, while the north face above Loch Bealach na h'Oidche is rocky enough to have given a rock-climb.

The mountain can be climbed easily, if steeply, from Arnisdale, possibly best by means of the remains of the path to Gleann Beag which leaves the road about $1\frac{1}{2}$ miles north-west of the village. This climbs up to the west ridge (An Sgriodhal – the O.S. seems to have had some spelling problems hereabouts!) which can be followed to the top, from which the view is very fine indeed. The drop from the summit to Loch Hourn represents 3196 ft. in 1 mile, equalling that on the south side of Sgurr na Ciste Duibhe on the Five Sisters of Kintail.

Several other routes to the summit offer to those who can study the one-inch map.

Mealfuarvonie, 2284 ft. – This hill, which stands on the west side of Loch Ness north of Invermoriston is very conspicuous in views along the Great Glen. As a result it is renowned far more than its climbing interest justifies. It has, however, the reputation of being the highest Old Red Sandstone mountain in the country.

Paths

Loch Quoich to Glen Shiel: Good paths lead from Alltbeithe in Glen Quoich and from Coireshubh on the Kinloch Hourn road to the Bealach Duibh Leac and Achnangart in Glen Shiel. Either makes a good pass-walk for car-swapping parties.

From Alltbeithe, too, a path to the west end of Loch Loyne gives access to some unmapped zig-zag paths on the south slopes if the South Glen Shiel Ridge.

Other paths relevant to this chapter are mentioned in Chapter 10.

9

Kintail

Sgurr Fhuaran, 3505 ft. (979167)
Sgurr na Carnach, 3270 ft. (977159)
Sgurr na Ciste Duibhe, 3370 ft. (984149)
Sgurr na Spainteach, 3129 ft. (993149)
Saileag, 3124 ft. (019147)
Sgurr a' Bhealaich Dheig, 3378 ft. (033143)
Sgurr an Fhuarail, 3241 ft. (049138)
Ciste Dhubh, 3218 ft. (062167)
Beinn Fhada, 3385 ft. (019192)
A'Ghlas-bheinn, 3306 ft. (008231)

Munro's Tables, section 8.

Maps : One-inch Ordnance Survey, 7th Series, Sheets 26 and 35. Half-inch Bartholomew latest edtion, Sheets 50 and 54.

The hills described in this section mostly lie between Glen Shiel on the south and Glen Affric–Glen Lichd on the north. However a short northerly diversion by Gleann Gaorsaic to the Fall of Glomach and Glen Elchaig allows the whole of the mountains of Kintail to be included.

To the west of An Caorunn Mor lies the long chain of mountains forming the north side of Strath Cluanie and Glen Shiel, stretching from Ciste Dubh on the east to Sgurr na Moraich on the west, a distance of about 8½ miles. South of Ciste Dubh the deep Bealach a' Choinich (1968 ft.) breaks the high-level continuity of the chain, but from there, its west end, the ridge does not fall below 2317 ft. at Bealach an Lapain west of Saileag. The five mountains of the ridge west of the latter peak stand up well from several viewpoints as the 'Five Sisters of Kintail'.

By the artificial boundary imposed on this chapter are brought in the interminable ridge of Ben Attow (or Beinn Fhada) – the long Mountain – on the north side of Glen Ling, and the rather forgotten 'Munro', A' Ghlas-bheinn, above Dorusduian, in Strath Croe.

The hills of the Inverinate Forest, between Loch Duich and Glen Elchaig form a curious upland area which culminates in a rather negligible mountain, Sgurr an Airgid (2757 ft.), but within which lie several quite attractive crags and knolls.

The Five Sisters have long been justly famous as one of the most elegant mountain groups in the Highlands, showing up especially well from the old road pass of the Mam Ratagain on the way to Glenelg. Probably it is because of the existence of this much travelled route that the hills became renowned so many years ago. With their companion massif of Ben Attow they now form one of the finest pieces of mountain landscape in the care of the National Trust for Scotland. They were in fact purchased with the aid of funds made available by the late P. J. H. Unna (a one-time President of the Scottish Mountaineering Club) who regarded them as his personal gift to the Trust. This gift was over and above his massive contributions in respect of the Trust's Mountain Country Fund and towards the purchase of Glencoe.

The Trust's Kintail property has been extended by a protrusion northwards towards Glen Elchaig on its north side, to include the Fall of Glomach, the highest single waterfall in Scotland, said to comprise 350 ft. in a single leap. (It is surpassed in total height by a fall in several leaps near the head of Loch Glencoul in Sutherland.)

The main historical associations of the area have already been described in Chapter 8 but Eilean Donan Castle merits a special mention. Set on its rocky half-tide promontory into Loch Duich at Dornie it must be one of Scotland's finest castle sites. It certainly is the most photographed of any in the Highlands! The building as at present seen was restored by fairly massive rebuilding in 1910 and is the Clan Macrae War Memorial. It has the odd distinction of having been bombarded by English frigates at the time of the abortive Spanish-assisted rising of 1719, after which it was blown up, leaving only a shell. The original castle was an old one, probably dating back to Alexander II of Scotland and is on the site of an even older vitrified fort.

The bridge over the mouth of Loch Long at Dornie has an opening span to permit puffers to sail up to Sallachy, but despite many visits and longer holidays in the area the writer has never seen it open! While a sea journey may therefore no longer be available it is well worth while to go up the loch side by car to Killilan. It is remarkably fiord-like, and at high tide its upper reaches appear to belong to a completely landlocked inland loch. By continuing up Glen Elchaig (permission on signing a book at Killilan House) the nearest approach to the (invisible) Fall of Glomach can be reached near Loch na Leitreach.

The new Kintail to Dornie road is a high-speed level highway. It represents no mean undertaking to bench the road in at Loch level but despite their respect for modern engineering those interested in a really superb mountain view will take the steep, hairpin-curved old road to Carr Brae, above the modern highway. The outlook from the parking place at the top, especially that over the Five Sisters, under no circumstances should be missed. For those wishing a more profitable entertainment, however, the Geological Survey Memoir to the area says that traces of silver were found in an old trial mine near Carr Farm on the main road. One could pass the time in a little prospecting!

The Five Sisters Ridge: Sgurr Fhuaran, 3505 ft., **Sgurr na Ciste Duibhe,** 3370 ft., etc. – This long range of mountains is also known as Beinn Mhor (the Big Mountain) in contrast to its neighbour Beinn Fhada (the Long Mountain) on the other side of Glen Lichd.

Although it is long, one only gets two Munros for one's efforts in traversing it, as against the seven on the South Glen Shiel Ridge, although many people take in others by continuing along the ridge to the east. As it is justly one of the most popular excursions in the Highlands, it merits a fairly detailed description.

Beginning from the west end the first point of interest is the rugged little peak of Sgurr an t-Searraich (1886 ft.) at the entrance to Glen Shiel. One mile to the east is Sgurr na Moraich (2780 ft.), a bold conical peak which is the first of the Five Sisters, and is really the beginning of the main ridge. From it the ridge bends south-east, and, after dipping down to a bealach (2428 ft.), rises up to the fine triple-headed peak of Sgurr nan Saighead (2987 ft.). This mountain has deep, precipitous corries to the north-east, enclosed by great slabby rocks descending right from the summit. Three-quarters of a mile farther on, the main ridge, after passing the Bealach Bhuidhe (2713 ft.), rises steeply up to the summit of Sgurr Fhuaran. This has a rather ragged precipice to the north-east, and to the west throws out a very prominent nose, which is conspicuous as seen from the entrance to Glen Shiel. The grassy slopes of the peak dipping right down to Glen Shiel are exceedingly steep.

From Sgurr Fhuaran a well-defined ridge runs out east for about a mile, and forms the north containing wall of the profound Coire Domhain. South of the summit of Sgurr Fhuaran the main ridge drops down very steeply to Bealach na Carnach (2856 ft.), and then rises fairly gradually as a rough ridge to the rocky cone of Sgurr na Carnach (3270 ft.). Turning south-east falls to the Bealach na Craoibhe (2783 ft.) and then rises very gradually to Sgurr na Ciste Duibhe which is a fine rocky peak with craggy faces to the north overlooking Coire Domhain. On the north side of the peak there is a curious false ridge with a rock-strewn hollow between it and the steep north face of the final peak.

Half a mile farther on along the main ridge rises the somewhat narrow peak of Sgurr nan Spainteach (3129 ft.), which has a fine cluster of rocks of no great size on its north side. It derives its name from the pass across the ridge, the Bealach nan Spainteach (2913 ft.), a ¼ mile east from Sgurr na Ciste Duibhe, named after the Spanish contingent at the Battle of Glen Shiel (see chapter 8).

The four last-mentioned peaks enclose the head of Coire Domhain, a remote place overhung by steep rocks extending from Sgurr na Carnach to Sgurr nan Spainteach. One mile east from the latter peak the range terminates at the Bealach an Lapain (2371 ft.), beyond which the ridge rises up to Saileag, the first of the Sgurr a' Bhealaich Dheirg group.

The slopes of the various peaks of the Five Sisters overlooking Glen Shiel, although mostly grass, are extremely steep. That from the summit of Sgurr na Ciste Duibhe to the River Shiel represents 3170 ft. in seven eighths of a mile – an average angle of nearly 40 degrees. It is said to be the longest slope of its angle in the country.

The Five Sisters ridge should be traversed from east to west, as in common with nearly all of the valley divides of the Western Highlands, the best views are always to the west. The Bealach an Lapain can be reached with surprising ease directly up the steep slope from the gap in the forestry plantations about a mile east from the Site of Battle in Glen Shiel (N.G.R. 007135). The descent can be by Coire na Criche between Sgurr nan Saighead and Sgurr na Moraich. If done in reverse, however, it is worth while going up over the little peak of Sgurr an t'Searraich from Shiel Bridge, a rather rocky way. The northern, or Glen Lichd side, corries of the Five Sisters group have slabby rocky faces, some of which give some climbing, mainly in winter. The rock is of the granulite variety and is not well suited to rock routes. For these climbs the Hadden-Woodburn Memorial Hut (Glenlicht House) is a convenient centre. It is operated by the Edinburgh University Mountaineering Club to whom application for use should be made.

Saileag, 3124 ft. **Sgurr a' Bealaich Dheirg,** 3378 ft. **Sgurr an Fhuarail,** 3241 ft. – These hills form the easterly continuation of the Five Sisters Ridge with which they should properly be grouped. Most parties make a two-day job of it, however, perhaps taking in Ciste Dubh to extend the second day.

They merit little special description except for a mention that Sgurr an Fhuarail has two summits, as indicated above, three eighths of a mile apart, the western one being the higher. Sgurr a' Bhealaich Dheirg has its summit about 50 yards north of the main ridge in what is reputed to be a fine situation. The present writer might have been able to confirm this had it not been misty at the time of his only visit.

All the hills can be climbed easily from the main road, taking due note of the forestry plantings as shown on the map. Some new growth does not significantly affect the position.

Ciste Dhubh, 3218 ft. – This mountain is separated from the ones described above by the deep Bealach a' Choinich (1968 ft.) which breaks the high level continuity of the long ridge on the north side of Glen Shiel, started by the Five Sisters. It consists of a long and fairly narrow ridge running north from the Bealach and on its west side slopes steeply, but grassily, to the Allt Cam-ban and the Glen Affric watershed.

The east side is more broken up. The final peak is quite rocky to the south-east and north-east but, like most of the cliffs in the area, consists of steep flaggy slabs without any climbing potential except for a conspicuous gully on the south-east face. This gave a snow climb, but is not a rock route.

The shortest route to the mountain is up the valley of An Caorunn Beag, from Cluanie Inn, to the Bealach a' Choinich. The steep west slopes have been known to avalanche under appropriate conditions.

Beinn Fhada, 3385 ft. – This hill lies on the north-east side of Glen Lichd and, as its name implies, is a 'Long Mountain'. Its ridge runs for nearly seven miles and for four of them does not fall below 2750 ft. The name is commonly written anglicized as Ben Attow, which is a rough phonetic rendering of the Gaelic and for some reason the mountain seems to be well enough known among non-climbers for it to be given in children's school atlases! This is perhaps because folk can pronounce it!

The main interest in the hill lies in its western third where the northern corries have good rock faces and the ridge is relatively narrow, but thereafter the crest widens and loses all interest making the level walk over the plateau of the Plaide Mor to the summit an interminable 1½ mile trudge. The writer has never had the energy to continue east over Sgurr a'Dubhdhoire (3014 ft. – unnamed on the O.S. map) much less to complete the long walk to the end of the rather better defined ridge above Glen Affric.

Probably the best way to appreciate the mountain is to see first its northern corries from below by going up Gleann Choinneachain from Dorusduain in Strath Croe by way of the path leading to the Bealach an Sgairne. Near the sharp zig-zags on the path shown on the O.S. map a branch, not shown, leads off up Coir'an Sgairne towards the Plaide Mor from which the main summit can be reached. Walk back to Dorusduain over the ridge.

The hill can of course be climbed easily from the Youth hostel at Alltbeithe in Glen Affric or from Camban, a habitable bothy on the Affric–Glen Lichd path.

The south-eastern slopes of the mountain are seamed by landslip fissures. Coire Caol, on the north has some fair rock or snow climbing.

A'Ghlas-bheinn, 3006 ft. – Nobody seems to have much enthusiasm for this mountain, which stands at the head of Strath Croe, its side seamed by deep gullies. It is perhaps best taken in on the return walk from the Fall of Glomach, over Meall Dubh, with the descent being made S.S.W. to the Bealach an Sgairne, thus avoiding forestry complications above Dorusduain.

Paths

The Circuit of Beinn Fhada: This is a highly recommended trip which takes one through the heart of Kintail. Go up Glen Lichd by the path shown on the one-inch map and go over the watershed into Glen Affric by way of the Fionngleann. Return to the north of Beinn Fhada by the Allt Gleann Gniomhaidh (floodable ford) and the Bealach an Sgairne. The best section is Glen Lichd with fine views of the Five Sisters Ridge near its head and a quite impressive situation as the track goes up the waterfall of the Allt Granda. The journey is about 16 miles in all.

Croe Bridge to the Fall of Glomach: Croe Bridge lies on the loop road round the head of Loch Duich beyond the Causeway. Reach Dorusduain in Strath Croe either by the spur road up the strath or by a signposted track from Morvich. From there the path leads up the Allt an Leoid Ghaineamhaich to the Bealach na Sroine (*c.* 1700 ft), from which it is $1\frac{1}{4}$ miles to the Fall. *This is the recommended route to Glomach.*

Ardelve to the Fall of Glomach: By public road up the west side of Loch Long to Killilan and thence by private road (along which permission to drive can be obtained by signing a book at Killilan House), to the west end of Loch na Leitreach.

The River Elchaig is crossed by the A. E. Robertson Memorial Bridge near the foot of the loch, and beyond this the right-of-way path crosses the Glomach by the National Trust's bridge and follows the steep slopes on its west bank to the Allt na Laoidhre at the foot of the Chasm. It is probably easier, however, to keep along the steep slopes on the east side of the Glomach, by a very narrow path, and, when nearly opposite the Allt na Laoidhre, cross the Glomach and join the first-mentioned path.

After crossing the Allt na Laoidhre the path leads steeply up a grassy nose, with a fine view of the Chasm to the left, and, on reaching the foot of a rocky face, strikes off across the steep and somewhat rugged slopes above the Chasm to the top of the Fall. The height of the Fall is stated to be about 350 ft. The depth of the Chasm, from the top of the rocks at the Fall to the junction of the Glomach with the Allt na Laoidhre, is 491 ft.

Despite the fact that access bridges have been constructed over the rivers this route is not recommended for those who have not a good head for heights. Care is needed in places and the path is disintegrating. The route from Croe Bridge (see above), though longer, traverses less steep ground.

Reference
P. J. H. Unna and the Mountainous Country Trust. Scottish Mountaineering Club Journal, Vol. 30, 1972.

10

Glen Affric and Glen Cannich

Mam Sodhail, 3862 ft. (120253)
Carn Eige, 3380 ft. (124262)
Tom a' Choinich, 3646 ft. (165273)
Toll Creagach, 3455 ft. (195283)
An Socach, 3017 ft. (089231)
Beinn Fhionnlaidh, 3294 ft. (116283)
Sgurr nan Ceathreamhnan, 3771 ft. (058228)
Creag a'Choir' Aird, *c.* 3210 ft. (082264)
Sgor na Diollaid, 2676 ft. (283363)
Creag Dubh, 3102 ft. (200351)
Carn nan Gobhar, 3251 ft. (182344)
Sgurr na Lapaich, 3775 ft. (161352)
An Riabhachan, 3696 ft. (134345)
An Socach, 3508 ft. (101334)

Munro's Tables, Section 8 and 9.

Maps: One-inch Ordnance Survey, 7th Series, Sheets 26, 27; Bartholomew latest
edition, Sheets 54, 55.

Glen Affric (or Affaric) and Glen Cannich are two of Scotland's most
celebrated valleys and, of them, Glen Affric is probably the most
renowned in the Highlands after Glen Coe. Unlike that stark pass,
however, Glen Affric is famous for its beauty, being claimed by many
as the loveliest in all Scotland. The present writer has his reservations
on this statement, but agrees that it must rank at least in the top three
or four.

Lovely it certainly is, but its beauty lies largely in its lower reaches,
in that part up to Lochs Beinn a'Mheadhoin (Benevean) and Affric
which are accessible to the general tourist. Beyond the head of the
latter loch, however, it becomes unremarkable except in respect of
its size.

In the lower part of the glen the road climbs up from Fasnakyle in
Strath Glass to follow along the tree-clad gorge of the Chisholm's
Pass, above the Dog Falls. Hereabouts a good number of old Scots
Pine trees still remain to dominate the view, competing on more than

98

equal terms with the Forestry Commission's lesser conifers. Beyond the Benevean Dam, however, the view opens out to provide some really fine prospects over the pine-clad shores and islands on Loch Beinn a'Mheadhoin towards the (rather too distant) hills. The public road ends a short distance from the west end of the loch, but even if you are not climbing, it is worth continuing on foot to Loch Affric, where the hills are closer and the spurs of the Mam Sodhail group tower grandly above fine stands of pine and the waters of the loch. Probably the best view is from the south side of the river, near the Lodge, on the Forestry Commission access road. One should beware of Indians hereabouts, the area being in demand among producers of TV plays as Britain's nearest approach to the Canadian woods.

Much of the south side of the glen is planted forest, through which many rough roads can be followed, as far (at the time of writing), as a short distance beyond the west end of Loch Affric, giving foot access to the valleys running up to A'Chralaig and Tigh Mor na Seilge. For the hills north side, the track past Affric Lodge on the north side of the Loch should be taken. This eventually reaches the Youth Hostel at Alltbeithe (Alltbeath) which, of course, is an excellent centre for the more remote hills at the glen head. At Alltbeithe the path branches, that to the north reaching Strath Croe by way of the Bealach an Sgairne, that to the south reaching Morvich (on Strath Croe) by way of Glen Lichd, passing an old bothy at Camban near the watershed about three miles from the Hostel. This bothy has recently been rendered habitable.

The more usual route to Alltbeithe, however, is by way of An Caorunn (or Caoruinn) Mor, from Glen Moriston, near Cluanie Inn, although the route has nothing at all to commend it except its relative shortness.

Glen Cannich is much less attractive, being more enclosed than is its strath-like southern neighbour, but, again, is impressive because of its sheer size and continuity. It lacks any really good mountain prospect, the view along it being made up largely of the terminations of the shoulders of the main peaks which lie well back above its steep sides. It is accessible by public road as far as the mighty Mullardoch Dam at the east end of the Mullardoch Reservoir. This sheet of water lies over the site of the former Loch Mullardoch and Loch Lungard and, on the whole, the author considers the view to have been enhanced by its presence. Others will argue this contention. It will henceforward be referred to as Loch Mullardoch.

Whatever the merits of the view, however, there can be no dis-agreement about the devastating effect of the reservoir construction on access to the hills hereabouts. The former road to Benula Lodge has been inundated and no replacement track has been constructed, although for some distance west of the dam a kind of ditch half-heartedly indicates the general line to follow. Even if this can be found it is of no help. The going is not too bad, however, until the Allt Taige is reached. Thereafter, until the track rises from the reservoir about $1\frac{1}{2}$ miles from its western end the going is absolutely terrible although the one-inch map insists that there is a path here-abouts. It is as well to remember this if you intend to complete a hard day's circuit by returning along the loch shore.

Parties may be able to hire a boat on the loch from one or other of the hotels in the area (*e.g.* Glen Affric Hotel, Cannich).

The contrasting attractions of the two glens have been made use of by the Hydro-Electric Engineers (see p. 26), who, although, it would probably have been economically better to enlarge Loch Beinn a'Mheadhoin still further, have preserved Glen Affric at the expense of Glen Cannich by making the main water storage in the latter valley. Water from Loch Mullardoch, conducted by tunnel under the valley-divide 'tops up' Loch Beinn a'Mheadhoin to such an extent that the fluctuation is only about 6 ft. in summer and about twelve in winter. For comparison the *natural* fluctuation of Loch Affric is about ten feet.

Naturally, to compensate for this a price has to be paid and Loch Mullardoch can develop a pretty large shore-line scar late in the year.

All the mountains of the area are massive and those whose main access is from Glen Affric or Glen Cannich are pretty remote, necessitating longish days in summer and speedy travel in winter. Being high and central they often carry a good deal of snow. Carn Eige (pronounced with a hard 'g') is in fact the highest summit north of the Caledonian Canal.

Although the main hills of the area lie within the belt of variable mica-schists and granulites from which many of the rugged peaks to the south are carved, their outline in this case are smooth and rounded rather than rough and sharp. Probably this is because of their more central position in the Western Highlands where, in glacial times, an ice cap could have existed to some extent protecting them during the stage of valley glaciation.

A surprising number of the mountains in this chapter have had their heights slightly altered on the latest edition of the 7th Series one-inch map, *e.g.* Carn Eige itself, now 3880 ft. (formerly 3877 ft.); Toll Creagach 3455 ft. (3452 ft.); Sgurr na Lapaich (north) 3775 ft. (3773 ft.); An Socach 3508 ft. (3503 ft.) and Braigh a'Choire Bhig has grown to a surprising 3317 ft. from a diminutive 3303 ft!

Although it is generally admitted that the continents are at present in an active state of movement over the earth's surface, these changes in height unfortunately do not indicate a rapid rise of Scotland's mountains towards the permanent snow-line. They in fact result from different standards used by the O.S. for the position at which these observations were taken. The same has happened on the new Tourist Edition of the Cairngorms area map. To a keen eye the corrections can be seen by a different type face used on the revised map where changes have been made. Afficionados of the subject will note that this plays havoc with the pecking order of Munro's Tables as An Socach now takes precedence over Sgurr Fhuaran and Braigh Choire Chruinn-bhalgain.

Mam Sodhail and Sgurr na Lapaich (north of Loch Mullardoch) were two important stations of the primary triangulation of Scotland in the 1840's. This accounts for the huge cairn on the former peak, which originally was 23 ft. in height. That in Sgurr na Lapaich (100 ft. W.S.W. of the highest point on the mountain was about 22 ft. high).

Mam Sodhail, 3862 ft. **Carn Eige**, 3880 ft. – These mountains are the twin summits of the large group of mountains which stand between the west end of Loch Affric and the head of Glen Cannich, and which is bounded on the west by Gleann a' Choitich and the Allt Coire Ghaidheil. Roughly, the group extends 5 miles from north to south and 7 miles from east to west. It contains four summits over 3000 ft., which are classified as separate mountains. With few exceptions, the individual members of the group are characterized by great flattish ridges and summit plateaus, somewhat resembling the Cairngorms in this respect.

The massif is best described as being a long ridge extending, from the Bealach Coire Ghaidheil (2350 ft.) in the west, in a north-east direction over Mam Sodhail to Carn Eige, a distance of about 2¼ miles, and then trending E.N.E. for 4½ miles to Toll Creagach, where it merges into the lower hills extending to the upper part of Strath Glass. For 6½ miles the ridge only falls below the level of 3000 ft., for a short break of about ¼ mile at the Bealach Toll Easa (2877 ft.), ½ mile east of Tom a' Choinich.

Because of the height of the main mountains, many of the supporting peaks and intermediate summits on the ridges exceed 3000 ft. and
are classified as 'Tops' in Munro's Tables. As not all are named on the
one-inch map (even one 'Munro' is missing) a fairly detailed description of the massif is useful.

In detail, the main ridge rises up steeply E. by N. from the Bealach
Coire Ghaidheil (2350 ft.) in $\frac{1}{2}$ mile to Carn Coulavie (point 3508 ft.
on the O.S. map called Stob Coire Coulavie by Munro), from which a
branch ridge runs S.S.E. in $\frac{1}{2}$ mile to an unnamed top (3462 ft.) above
Creag a' Chaoruinn whose name Munro has given to the summit
itself. Continuing along the main ridge, the next top, $\frac{1}{2}$ mile north-
east, is Ciste Dhubh (3606 ft. also without name on the one-inch
map), from near which a branch ridge runs out one mile south-east to
a top (c. 3500 ft.), called Saoiter Mor on the six-inch map but which
is called An Tudair on the one-inch edition. Half a mile beyond Ciste
Dubh, the flat and stony main ridge rises up to the summit of Mam
Sodhail, which is crowned by a very large cairn. The $2\frac{1}{4}$ mile ridge
running out south-east from Mam Sodhail over the small top of
Mullach Cadha Rainich (3262 ft.) to Sgurr na Lapaich (3401 ft.) is of
the same character as the main ridge, but on the east face of Lapaich
there are some steep rocks.

From the summit of Mam Sodhail a $\frac{1}{2}$ mile ridge leads north, and
then N.N.E., to the top of Carn Eige, with steep, rocky slopes on the
east dropping down to the small Loch Uaine (c. 2950 ft.). The gap
in the main ridge above it, between the two summits, is 3429 ft.

From Carn Eige the main ridge runs E.N.E. in $\frac{1}{2}$ mile to Creag na
h-Eige (3753 ft.), east of which the ridge becomes much narrower,
and in another $\frac{1}{2}$-mile reaches Stob Coire Domhain (3725 ft.), and
three-eighths of a mile farther on Sron Gharbh (3705 ft.). At one
point the ridge is quite narrow, with several small pinnacles or needles
of rock, which can be by-passed. This section is entertaining in
winter. The drop eastwards from Sron Gharbh to the Garbh-
bhealach (3159 ft.) is steep and shows the remains of a stone staircase
which was built many years ago for the convenience of sportsmen. In
winter this needs care. From Sron Gharbh the ridge trends north-
east for $1\frac{1}{2}$ miles to Tom a' Choinich (3646 ft.), before reaching which
the ridge passes over 2 small tops called An Leth-Chreag (3443 ft.)
and Tom a' Choinich Beag (3384 ft.). The ridge then drops down, in
$\frac{1}{2}$ mile, to the Bealech Toll Easa (2877 ft.) at the head of the Allt Lub
nam Meann. (From here a good path leads south to Gleann nam

Fiadh.) Beyond the Bealach the ridge rises up gradually to the summit of Toll Creagach, which has already been described. Affric Lodge may be reached from Gleann nam Fiadha by crossing a bridge ¼ mile west of the Allt Toll Easa junction and following a path leading south over the shoulder of Am Meallan.

From the summit of Carn Eige an important ridge runs out N.N.W. for 1½ miles to Beinn Fhionnlaidh (3294 ft.) which, believe it or not, is usually referred to as (phonetically) 'Benully'. This suggests that its true name was at one time Beinn na h' Udhlaidh (the hill of the treasure).

The ridge of the massif can be reached by any one of several paths shown on the one-inch map, but the hills, omitting Beinn Fionn-laidh, are probably most easily climbed from Glen Affric by way of the Amhuinn Gleann nam Fiadha at the end of the public road. From the parking place, that glen and the track up the Allt Toll Easa should be followed to the Bealach Toll Easa, east of Tom a'Choinich. The main ridge can then be followed over Carn Eige to Mam Sod-hail and continued westwards as far as one wants, possibly to Bealach Coire Ghaidheil.

New plantings seem to be projected in Gleann nam Fiadh but the access road for them should still provide a way to the track farther up the glen and to that up the Allt Toll Easa.

Beinn Fhionnlaidh, formerly easily reached from the Mullardoch side, is now a very inaccessible mountain. The best way of reaching it would be to take it in as part of a main ridge trip.

For a relatively short day a recommended trip is to climb Sgurr na Lapaich by the path which goes first due north and then west from Affric Lodge. Cross the Allt na Faing west of the sharp angle of the path at about 1900 ft. and make a way, as seems suitable, to the summit. Then follows a very pleasant high level walk to Mam Sodhail from whence Carn Eige can be traversed to Sron Garbh. In snow the descent down the south-east ridge of the latter hill could be easier than the summer route *via* the Garbh-bealach.

Toll Creagach, 3455 ft. – This hill is really the eastward continua-tion of the Carn Eige–Tom a'Choinich ridge but as most people will have had enough by the time the Bealach Toll Easa is reached it is most often climbed separately. It is probably best reached by way of Gleann nam Fiadh from the car park at the end of Loch Benevean, but pro-jected new planting may make a roundabout circuit necessary by way of the Allt Toll Easa and the Bealach. Choose the way accordingly.

The hills of the *Ceannacroc Forest* (Chapter 8) can all be reached from Glen Affric by way of Gleann na Ciche which leads off to the south from the west end of Loch Affric, but their ascent from this side is not particularly interesting. The slopes on this approach are pretty smooth and the outlook not as good as one might expect from the fine views from Loch Affric side. Forestry work is planned for the lower reaches of this glen and may be in hand by the time of publication of this book.

Sgurr nan Ceathreamhnan, 3771 ft. – This mountain is the highest point of the considerable massif which lies west of Bealach Coire Ghaidheil and on the west is bounded by Gleann Gaorsaic. It is the fourth in order of height of all the mountains north of the Great Glen. It has two summits, west (37736 ft.) and east (3771 ft. – the main top).

From the west summit four ridges radiate. The north ridge runs out over Stuc Mor (*c.* 3496 ft.) to Stuc Bheag (*c.* 3250 ft.), one mile north of the west summit, where it splits into two shoulders enclosing the Loch an Fhraoich-choire (*c.* 2540 ft.). The north-west ridge is $\frac{3}{4}$ mile long, and terminates at Creag nan Clachan Geala (3282 ft.). The south ridge leads towards Beinn an t-Socach on the north side of Gleann Gniomhaidh, and the east ridge, of course, leads to the highest summit of the mountain. From the latter, a ridge leads in a north-easterly direction, in $\frac{3}{4}$ mile, to the Bealach nan Daoine (*c.* 2757 ft.) at the beginning of the long Creag a' Choir' Aird ridge, which is about $2\frac{1}{2}$ miles in length, and does not fall below 3000 ft. for quite 2 miles. The highest point of the ridge is near the north end and about $\frac{1}{2}$ mile south of the O.S. cairn (3188 ft.), and apparently about 30 ft. higher. The height of the summit of the hill is therefore regarded as being approximately 3210 ft.

From the main summit, again, an important ridge leads almost due east for one mile to Stob Coire nan Dearcag (3089 ft.), and then continues as the watershed between Glen Affric and Glen Cannich for 1 mile to An Socach (3017 ft.), and beyond the latter north-east for $\frac{3}{4}$ mile, to the Bealach Coire Ghaidheil (2350 ft.) and the beginning of the Mam Sodhail group.

The pronunciation of the name Sgurr nan Ceathreamhnan always causes heated discussion. Very approximately it is 'Cerranan', but it does not matter, as the locals have another name for it (which the writer, unfortunately, failed to take a note of) and would probably fail to recognize even a correct Gaelic rendering of the word!

Whatever you call it, however, it is worth climbing as it has a

35. Glen Shiel. Faochag to the left, the Saddle to the right.

36. A'Chralaig from Mam Cluanie. A' Chralaig to the right. Sgurr nan Ceathreamhnan in centre. The sharp peak of Ciste Dhubh on left, just showing to the left of the top of Am Bathach. *A. E. Robertson*

37. The South Glen Shiel Ridge. Summer.

38. The South Glen Shiel Ridge. Winter. From Sgurr a'Mhaoraich.

39. The Saddle from Sgurr na Sgine. The Sgurr nan Forcan Ridge to the right.

40. The Saddle. The summit ridge in winter (note the two climbers).

41. The Saddle from above Shiel Bridge. The Sgurr nan Forcan Ridge to the left, Spidean Dhomhuill Bhric to the right.

42. Broch, Gleann Beag, Glenelg.

43. Beinn Sgritheall from Arnisdale.

44. The Five Sisters Ridge. Beinn Fhada behind.

dominating position, with good views. Unless you are staying at the Youth Hostel the easiest way to get to it is from the Glomach Chasm, reached by driving up Glen Elchaig (permission on signing a book at Killilan House) to the A. E. W. Robertson Memorial Bridge at the south-west end of Loch na Leitreach. From the top of the Fall a choice of easy routes to the summit is open. The most direct is up the north-west ridge over Creag na Clachan Geala (not named on the one-inch map). If time and car-ferrying wife (or husband) is available, a very pleasant and highly recommended route of return is over Sgurr Gaorsaic (c. 2600 ft.) to the Bealach an Sgairne and thence to Dorus-dain at the head of Strath Croe in Kintail. By this means some spectacular scenery is taken in. The hardy can take in Creag a'Choir'Aird as well and this has been done, Dorusdain and return, *via* the Fall of Glomach.

THE GLEN CANNICH HILLS

Sgor na Diollaid, 2676 ft. – This is the culminating point of the eastern end of the long range of low hills that separate Glen Cannich and Glen Strathfarrar. Its rocky top is a conspicuous landmark from the lower reaches of these glens, but gives no real climbing. It is most easily climbed from Glen Cannich, which should be left at the bridge just beyond Muchrachd. The actual summit of the hill is a crest of rocky knobs about 260 yds long, the highest points being at the northern end. A complete traverse of the ridge gives a rocky scramble without any real difficulty.

Carn nan Gobhar, 3251 ft. **Creag Dhubh,** 3102 ft. – These are two rather featureless hills that rise on the north side of Loch Mull-ardoch, and really form the eastern termination of the Sgurr na Lapaich (Ross) group. The most convenient route of ascent is from the end of the road at the Mullardoch Dam from which the round of the two hills is straightforward, and somewhat uninteresting. Note that the cairn on Carn nan Gobhar is 200 yds south of the true summit, and about 40 ft lower than it.

Sgurr na Lapaich, 3775 ft. **An Riabhachan,** 3696ft. **An Socach,** 3508 ft. – Sgurr na Lapaich is the highest peak of the long range of mountains which divide Glen Strathfarrar from Glen Cannich, and extend westwards to the head of Glen Elchaig. An Riabhachan adjoins it to the west, and is the highest mountain in Ross-shire. The west end of the range is called An Socach and is not named on the one-inch map.

Sgurr na Lapaich is the finest, as well as the highest, member of the group. It stands on the north side of Loch Mullardoch, towards which it throws out a ridge containing two well-defined tops: Sgurr nan Clachan Geala (*c*. 3591 ft.), a little over ½ mile S. by E. from the summit, and Braigh a' Choire Bhig (3317 ft.), ½ mile south-west father along the ridge. (The O.S. map gives this name to the whole southern ridge.) A ¼ mile north of the summit there is a small top called Rudha na Spreidhe (*c*. 3484 ft.), beyond which the north slopes of the mountain fall easily to Gleann Innis an Loichel. There are two very fine corries on the south-east aspect of the mountain, separated by a ridge running south-east from Sgurr nan Clachan Geala to the top of Creag a' Chaoruinn (*c*. 3195 ft.), at the end of the ridge. Each corrie contains a small loch, that in the south corrie being called Loch a' Choire Bhig, and the other Loch Tuill Bhearnach. The north-west face of Sgurr na Lapaich and the headwall of the corrie containing Loch Tuill Bhearnach are steep and rocky, but give no rock climbs.

To the south-west, Sgurr na Lapaich drops down pretty steeply to the Bealach Toll an Lochain (*c*. 2650 ft.), beyond which a somewhat interesting ridge rises up to the east end of the long summit ridge of An Riabhachan. The north-east slopes of this eastern ridge of An Riabhachan, called Creagan Toll an Lochain, are very steep and rocky, and dip down to two little lochs, Loch Mor and Loch Beag. The highest point of An Riabhachan (3696 ft.) is about three-eighths of a mile W.S.W. from the top of the east ridge, and beyond it the main ridge is almost level, for nearly a mile, to the west summit (3559 ft.). With the exception of the east ridge, and the north-east slopes above the two little lochs, An Riabhachan is an uninteresting mountain with grassy slopes on all the other sides.

From the west summit the hill drops down, in five-eighths of a mile, to the Bealach a' Bholla (2956 ft.), and then rises up to the summit of An Socach (3508 ft.), ¾ mile farther on. After that the mountain drops down westwards to the valley leading from Loch Monar to Glen Elchaig. From the summit of An Socach, a ridge runs south-east to its lower summit, from which a rather narrow and steep buttress drops into the eastern corrie. The climb up this buttress is quite easy, and is an interesting way up the hill.

These mountains are a long distance from anywhere, and are, therefore, difficult of access. This is especially true of An Socach and An Riabhachan, now that the driving road along the north side of Loch Mullardoch has been inundated, together with the Mullardoch–

Iron Lodge path. The easiest way to get to them is from the Mullardoch Dam and along the north bank of the reservoir, keeping fairly high, to a bridge over the Allt Mullardoch. From there the going is not too bad until a good path is met leading up the east bank of the Allt Taige. Follow this to the burn junction about 1 mile from the loch and climb easily up the south-east ridge of Lapaich, over Sgurr nan Clachan Geala, to the summit. The main ridge can then be followed westwards over the remarkably level tops of An Riabhachan to An Socach.

There is now no alternative but to descend to Loch Mullardoch side and thence back to the Allt Taige by what the O.S. misguidedly records as a path.

From the Strathfarrar side the hills can be climbed from Inchvuilt, first up the construction access road along the Uisge Misgeach, then by the continuation path to Clach an Daimh. The road or path can be left at a convenient point depending on the objective, say by the Garbh Choire and the east ridge for Lapaich or the branch path to Meall Garbh for An Riabhachan. If the traverse is continued to An Socach, probably the best method of return is back over the flat ridge of An Riabhachan, although this involves a re-ascent of about 600 ft. from the Bealach a'Bolla. Do not go down to Beallach Toll an Lochan in winter unless you have previously worked out a route of descent from there to the corrie. (See Rock Climbs section.)

If the An Socach–An Riabhachan ridge is the sole object of your desires to complete your bag of Munros then it appears that the quickest access is from the west, up Glen Elchaig by car (permission at Killilan Lodge as on (page 97), with a request to go as far as you are willing to drive past Loch na Leitreach). With luck you might get to Iron Lodge, from which An Socach could probably be reached either by the remaining section of the Mullardoch path, or that past Loch Mhoicean.

An Cruachan, 2312 ft. – Out of the desolate country between An Socach and Lurg Mhor rises An Cruachan which were it not for geologists would be surely one of the least ascended hills of its height in the country. It has some unusual rocks for the area, including a variety containing graphite. It is usually reached from Iron Lodge, in Glen Elchaig.

Paths

Hill paths between Glen Affric and Glen Cannich: Two hill paths are
shown on the one-inch map traversing the country between the two
glens, one over the Bealach Coire Ghaidheill, the other over the
Bealach Toll Easa. These were formerly useful cross-country routes
but since the enlargement of Loch Mullardoch now serve only as
access to the hills (see p. 100). If you are using them for inter-valley
traverses note that there are no paths or bridges along the south side
of Loch Mullardoch.

Glen Cannich to Dornie: To the Mullardoch Dam and thence to the
Allt Coir' a'Mhaim as described for Sgurr na Lapaich and An Socach.
The author has not traversed the section from there to where the old
path rises from the loch to carry on to Iron Lodge, but his colleagues
tell him that it too, is heavy going. From Iron Lodge a rough road
leads to Loch na Leitreach in Glen Elchaig, where a car could meet
the party (see p. 100).

Upper Strath Glass and the Lochs: There is a plexus of paths
between upper Strath Glass and Loch Beinn a'Mheadhoin. These
are shown on the one-inch maps and many pleasant walks can be had,
mostly passing for a greater or lesser length in forest of one sort or
another. Many tracks are in fact Forestry Commission access roads
through plantings not yet shown on the one-inch maps. A choice
can be made to suit.

A specially recommended walk, however, is the circuit of Loch
Affric from and to the Forestry bridge about 1 mile east of Affric
Lodge. There is a bridge at Athnamulloch 1 mile west of the west end
of the loch.

Hill Paths between Strath Glass and Glen Moriston: From Tomich,
Glen Moriston may be gained by the track following the power lines.
This is reached from Hilton Cottage, near Guisachan House and
enters Glen Moriston at Torgyle Bridge.

Alternatively, but much more deviously, reach Ceannacroc by way
of Garve Bridge, Cougie and the Allt Riabhach to the River Doe.

These paths are shown on the one-inch map. They have little to
recommend them except in the Strath Glass stretch, but they could
be of interest to off-the-piste enthusiasts.

11

Glen Strathfarrar, Monar
and Strathconon

Beinn a'Bha'ach Ard, 2826 ft. (361434)
Sgurr na Ruaidhe, 3254 ft. (289426)
Carn nan Gobhar, 3235 ft. (273438)
Sgurr a'Choire Ghlais, 3554 ft. (259430)
Creag Ghorm a'Bhealaich, 3378 ft. (245435)
Sgurr Fhuar-thuill, 3439 ft. (235438)
Sgurr na Fearstaig, 3226 ft. (227438)
Sgurr na Muice, 2915 ft. (226418)
Maoile Lunndaidh, 3295 ft. (135458)
Bidean an Eoin Deirg, 3430 ft. (104442)
Sgurr a'Chaorachain, 3455 ft. (088447)
Sgurr Choinnich, 3260 ft. (076447)
Lurg Mhor, 3234 ft. (065404)
Bidean a'Choire Sheasgaich, 3102 ft. (050413)
Sguman Coinntich, 2881 ft. (977304)
Sgurr a' Mhuilinn, 2883 ft. (260558)
Moruisg, 3033 ft. (103502)

Munro's Tables, Section 9.

Maps: One-inch Ordnance Survey 7th Series, Sheets 26, 27. Half-inch Bartholomew latest edition, Sheets 54, 55.

North of Glen Cannich the east-west through-valley system of the Western Highlands becomes less defined, the western end of Strathfarrar entering into an area of complex topography around the headwaters of the River Ling while Glen Orrin just fails to cut through the ridge north of Loch Monar, so terminating without a through route at its head. Strathconon and the River Meig do link up to the west with the valley of the Allt a'Chonais (sometimes called Glen Uig) to reach Strath Carron near Achnashellach but do so in an irregular zig-zag manner unlike the through routes to the south. In addition Strath Carron lies transverse to the east-west line rather than continuing it.

As most of the interesting mountains left to be described in the Western Highlands District lie in this complex country round the valley heads and not in the glens themselves, they will be described together in one chapter, following the precedent of the original District Guide. The area thus includes all the Western Highlands north of a line which runs from Glen Strathfarrar south-west from Patt Lodge on Loch Monar, to Glen Elchaig by way of the desolate depression between An Riabhachan and the hills of the Killilan Forest, and so reaches Loch Long and Dornie.

This is in fact a very well marked valley system forming a pass through the Highlands long used as a trade-route. Its highest point is only *c.* 1450 ft. at Loch Mhoicean near Iron Lodge at the head of Glen Elchaig. It is (or was) a right of way readily negotiable until the enlargement of Loch Monar cut across it at Patt Lodge, leaving a long trackless section to be negotiated along the Loch side (p. 116). What its present status is just now is not known.

Access to the area is of course rather diverse. For Glen Strathfarrar a private road leads to the Monar Dam at the east end of the enlarged Loch Monar. There is a locked gate at the eastern (Strath Glass) end. This has an ingenious multiple lock system – one for each of the estates which the Glen traverses – but fortunately unlocking any one undoes the chain. Permits for this to be effected can be had at the time of writing at an estate office at Struy at the road end or at the estate offices at the Royal Bank in Beauly. The relatively easy access now permitted is a great help to climbers. The privilege should not be abused.

Glen Orrin is only accessible as far as the Orrin Dam a few miles from its eastern end. The new reservoir floods back for about $4\frac{1}{2}$ miles over what was a pretty cheerless valley, inundating the old track but fortunately Glen Orrin never served as a main access to any hill of interest.

Strathconon (the name seems only to apply to the lower reaches of the Meig valley) is accessible by car from Marybank near Strathpeffer to Scardroy Lodge. At one time it served as the trade route to Loch Maree and the west, before the opening of the Dingwall–Kyle of Lochalsh railway. Osgood Mackenzie describes one such family journey to Poolewe, by way of Scardroy and from thence to Ach-nasheen!

Access from the west will be described with the mountain details later on.

Glen Strathfarrar is an attractive valley, with a fair amount of wooded country containing Scots Pine trees. Even where it opens out in its upper reaches the hills are not scenically too remote, although giving full measure to the immensity of the glen. As far as one can go by car, the hydro-electric works are not obtrusive, but the great arch dam (p. 26) impounding Loch Monar puts a sudden stop to the wilderness character of the upper reaches.

Strathconon is also very attractive, especially in that area about the lower reaches around Torrachilty. It remains so until Milltown but thereafter loses its charm. That section from Milltown to Invercharan is remarkably straight, as the valley follows the line of the great Strathconon Fault, one of Scotland's major fracture-lines.

Despite several attempts to visit the Strathfarrar hills and the Maoile Lunndaidh area especially for this Guide the author has always been frustrated in his attempts – usually because of the weather! Sections dealing with these mountains are therefore based directly on the account by the author of the previous District Guide.

The Strathfarrar Hills; Sgurr a'Choire Ghlais, 3554 ft. **Beinn a'Bha'ach Ard,** 2827 ft., etc. – These hills run east and west along the north side of Glen Strathfarrar. Beinn a'Bha'ach Ard (whose height has been revised on the 7th Series map) and Sgurr a' Phollain (2773 ft.) lie at the eastern end of the ridge. The former forms a fine cone-chaped peak, which is conspicuous in the view from Inverness or from the Beauly Firth. Westwards from Sgurr a' Phollain the watershed ridge is smooth and grassy over Meallan Buidhe (2503 ft.) to Sgurr na Ruaidhe (3254 ft.) which is the start of a major group of hills above the west end of Loch Monar. These comprise the major attraction of the Glen.

South from the summit of Sgurr na Ruaidhe lies the rocky summit of Garbh-charn (2801 ft.) but its own top is flat and uninteresting. continuing westwards the main ridge dips down to the Bealach nam Bogan (2521 ft.) then rises to Carn nan Gobhar (formerly 3242, but now 3255 ft.) the summit of which is covered with loose stones and has steep grassy slopes to the north. The grassy main ridge then leads south-west to the next bealach (2833 ft.), then rises westwards to the graceful peak of Sgurr a'Choire Ghlais.

Beyond Sgurr a' Choire Ghlais there is a dip of some 600 feet to the next bealach (2964 ft.), and then comes Sgurr Fhuar-thuill, which is a long ridge, a mile in length, running east and west with three tops: Creag Ghorm a'Bhealaich (3378 ft.) at the east end, Sgurr Fhuarthuill (3439 ft.) in the centre, and Sgurr na Fearstaig (3326 ft.) at the west end. These three summits are all pretty much of the same character, with craggy faces overlooking the deep corries on the northern side of the ridge; but possessing no outstanding structural features.

From Sgurr na Fearstaig a spur runs south, at right angles to the main ridge, the eastern side of which is far wilder and more rocky than any part of the main ridge. Sgurr na Muice (2915 ft.), 1¼ miles to the south, rises in an almost unbroken precipitous face above the deep corrie of Loch Toll a' Mhuic; and Beinn na Muice (2272 ft.), at the south end of the spur, presents bare rocky slopes to the east and south. Between these two peaks is the little Carn an Daimh Bhain (2043 ft.).

Beinn a'Bha'ach Ard can be climbed easily from Culligran by way of either the east or west corries (paths for some distance shown on the map), or by the bare rocky shoulder between them which falls into Strathfarrar. For Sgurr na Ruaidhe and points west the track up from Deanie can be taken. In mist the section between that mountain and Carn nan Gobhar might need some navigation, but thereafter the ridge is defined. After passing Sgurr na Muice drop down east at the first convenient point and join the Allt Toll a'Mhuic path.

There is some rock-climbing to be had on the Loch Toll a' Mhuic corrie.

Maoile Lunndaidh, 3295 ft. – This is a large, massive mountain which stands on the north side of Loch Monar and overlooks Gleann Fhiodhaig to the north. The summit ridge is about 1 mile in length and has 3 tops, which, however are separated by very slight dips. The centre top (3295 ft.) is the summit of Creag Toll a' Choin, the crags surrounding the deep corrie of that name on the south-east side of the mountain. It is the highest point on the hill and Munro's Tables in fact give 'Creag Toll a' Choin' as the 'Munro'. The O.S. summit (3294 ft.) is the 'Maoile Lunndaidh' of Munro's Tables and is thus only a 'Top'. This may be strictly correct, but common usage assigns the latter name to the mountains as a whole. The O.S. top lies about ½ mile north-east of Creag Toll a' Choin and is rather featureless. W.N.W. from Creag Toll a' Choin the ridge runs for ½ mile to the third top, Carn nam Fiaclan (3253 ft.). The finest feature of the mountain is the little corrie – the Fuartholl Mor – on the N.N.W. side of the hill. It is a deep-cut trench overlooked by the ridge connecting the three summits of the mountain. It contains three small Lochans, one above the other, and some interesting rocks. The Toll a' Choin, on the opposite side of the summit ridge, is fringed by some very fine crags. With the exception of these two corries the slopes of the mountain are mostly grassy and uninteresting.

46. Ciste Dubh. The summit ridge.

47. The Fall of Glomach.

48. Loch Affric from near Affric Lodge. Sgurr na Lapaich above. *W. S. Thomson*

49. Loch Mullardoch. Beinn Fhionnlaidh on left with the Braigh a'Choire Bhig ridge of Sgurr na Lapaich on right. The loch is now enlarged and reaches nearly up to the wood in the middle distance (in this picture it is aarely to ... ised over) W. S. Thomson

The mountain is rather inaccessible. The usual route is from the Strath Carron (or Glen Carron) side up the valley of the Allt a' Chonais to Glenuaig Lodge. At the time of writing there is no objection to climbers following this access route (except during times of sporting or other estate activity) provided permission is sought at Craig or at Glencarron Lodge. (It might be possible to arrange use of the road through the new Forestry plantings until it becomes too rough in about $1\frac{1}{2}$ miles.) Half a mile short of the Lodge leave for the foot of the stream coming down from the Fuar-tholl Mor. Cross it and strike up the north-west slope of Maoile Lunndaidh, to the 3294-ft. top, and then continue over the highest point to the top of Carn nam Fiaclan. A simple walk down the north-west slope of the latter takes one back to the Glenuaig Lodge road.

The mountain may also be climbed from Scardroy, at the west end of Loch Beannacharain at the head of Strathconon, where the public road ends. From Scardroy follow the River Meig to the Allt an Amise and strike up the latter to the watershed, from which climb the east ridge of the mountain.

Bidean an Eoin Deirg, 3430 ft. **Sgurr a'Chaorachain,** 3452 ft. **Sgurr Choinnich,** 3260 ft. – These mountains lie to the north of the west end of Loch Monar, but since the enlargement of that loch and the inundation of part of the former path they are best reached from Glen Carron.

Bidean an Eoin Deirg stands at the east end of the group and is the finest of them, being a sharp peak with an imposing north-east corrie with some good rocks. Sgurr a'Chaorachain, whose height has been revised on the current one-inch map, has no particular features of remark but the north face of Sgurr Choinnich is a fine corrie with several buttresses.

To reach these hills from Glen Carron go up the Allt a'Chonais Glen as for Maoile Lunndaidh, to about a mile from Glenuaig Lodge. Cross the lower part of the Sron na Frianich and go up the An Cromallt to the bealach at the head of the Amhainn Strath Mhuilich. From it climb up the north face of Bidean an Eoin Deirg, which is pretty steep, the main ridge being then followed westwards, as already described. A simpler route, which avoids the steep north face of Bidean and involves little additional climbing, is to make for the top of Sgurr a'Chaorachain first, and from it walk out to the top of Bidean an Eoin Deirg and back again. The total distance is just the same.

Lurg Mhor, 3234 ft. **Bidean a'Choire Sheasgaich,** 3102 ft. –

This is a very inaccessible group of hills lying to the west of Loch Monar, and 8 miles east of the head of Loch Carron. Lurg Mhor is a long, flat-topped ridge running westwards for about 4 miles from the head of Loch Monar, with easy slopes descending to the south. The north slope is very steep and precipitous, but without any good climbing rock. The mountain has two tops, the lower (3190 ft.) being ½ mile east of the highest point; the intervening dip is about 150 ft. and the connecting ridge has one rather awkward passage which is not readily avoidable.

Bidean a'Choire Sheasgaich is separated from Lurg Mhor by a deep bealach (c. 2421 ft.). It is a thin ridge running N.N.E. and shows up from north or south as a very sharp peak. Towards the north it throws out a narrow and in places very steep buttress or ridge above the Bealach an Sgoltaidh, from which the ascent requires care to a small perched lochan. (An accident hereabouts one winter only had a timely rescue as the result of a quite fortuitous appearance of a pass-walker. Nobody knew the climbers were in the district, much less on the hill!)

Any route to these hills involves a long walk. The usual way is to reach the west side of the group either by the rough (private) road from Attadale House on the south-east side of Loch Carron to Bendronaig Lodge or by the hill path from Achintee near Strathcarron Station. This is shown on the one-inch map and note that the Amhainn Bhearnais has to be forded. Bidean a'Choire Sheasgaich can then be climbed either by the Bealach an Sgoltaidh or, without difficulty, over Sail Riabach.

For most people camping would be needed, and if this is considered then an approach up the River Ling from Killilan might be thought of. There is a (private) rough road as far as Coire Domhain (*pron.* 'Dawn') and a track on the opposite bank of the Ling to Bendronaig Lodge. Alternatively reach Patt Lodge on Loch Monar, possibly by the Uisge Misgeach path (p. 116).

In any case the mountains are not for small parties without a return schedule arrangement with someone. The area is unfrequented and remote.

Sguman Coinntich, 2883 ft. – South of Lurg Mhor there lies a very desolate stretch of loch and peat bounded to the south-west by some featureless hills of which An Cruachan (p. 107) is the highest. To the south-west, however, the hills of Killilan Forest between Glen Ling and Glen Elchaig have more to recommend them. From Ben

Killilan (2466 ft.) on the west to Faochaig (2847 ft.) on the east they form a sinuous high level ridge with steep northern slopes, especially those around the deep subsidiary upper corries of Coire Domhain. Sguman Coinntich lies on a spur ridge, about midway in the group, and this ridge itself has a fine northern precipice above Coire Mhoir. The crags consist of steep but discontinuous slabs and offer no rock routes. In winter there would be avalanche danger here.

Sguman Coinntich can be approached fairly easily from Killilan by way of a steep, straight, unrelenting path up Coire Mhoir. From the upper corrie the mountain can be traversed, probably best from east to west as way down the steep slopes above Bealach Mhic Beathain might not be too obvious on the descent.

The mountain is relatively high and isolated and so it has an extensive view, except to the E.N.E. where Faochaig intervenes. Bidean a 'Choire Sheasgaich, especially, appears as a remarkably sharp peak from this angle.

Sgurr a'Mhuilinn, 2883 ft. – This many-peaked hill is gradually attaining the status of a mountain, having apparently grown no less than 38 ft. between editions of this guide. Its former height, on the Popular Edition map, was 2845 ft. It is a conspicuous feature, even being prominent from Ben Macdhui (or Macdui or Beinn Mac Duibh, depending on which O.S. spelling you prefer on the Tourist map of the Cairngorms), 58 miles away.

The mountain stands due west of Milltown in Strathconon and it has no less than six more or less well-defined summits of which five are named on the one-inch map. The missing one lies about $1\frac{1}{4}$ miles W.N.W. from Sgurr a'Mhuilinn and is apparently higher than its neighbouring Sgurr a'Ghlas Leathaid (2778 ft.). It is called Sgurr a'Choire Rainich.

The simplest way up Sgurr a'Mhuilinn is from Milltown and the mountain has a fine general view of the Ross-shire Peaks. Probably the most interesting way down would be to drop south-west to the bealach above Loch Coir' a'Mhuilinn and traverse Meallan Uan and Creag Ruadh, but of course other tops can be taken in as desired. Creag Ghlas, above Gleann Meinich is a bold crag on which some rock routes have been made, but the way from it to Sgurr a'Mhuilinn crosses some very haggy peat.

The route to the hill from Achanalt on the north cannot be recommended.

Moruisg, 3033 ft. – This massive and not very inspiring mountain lies on the south side of Glen Carron between Achnasheen and Achnashellach. Its main top lies on its central, northern spur due south of Loch Sgamhain. According to Munro's Tables the O.S. height (3026 ft.) differs from the six-inch map height quoted above, but the writer cannot say if the lack of revision on the present one-inch edition means that the six-inch value is suspect. Other summits are Carn Gorm (2866 ft.), 2 miles east of the main summit (note the O.S. trig point of 2843 ft. shown on the map a short distance to the north-east) and Sgurr nan Ceanraichean (2986 ft.), $1\frac{3}{4}$ miles south-west of the main summit. Towards Glen Carron the mountain shows a steep and unrelieved grassy slope descending from the summit to the valley; but east of the summit and stretching towards Carn Gorm there is a huge corrie drained by the Allt Gharagain containing two small lochs, Loch Cnoc na Mointeich and Loch Coireag nam Mang. The upper slopes of this corrie are very steep and much broken up, and might afford scope for snow climbing in spring. To the west of the summit there is another pronounced corrie, Coire Toll nam Bian, lying on the north-west side of the ridge running out towards Sgurr nan Ceanraichean. The south slopes of the mountain overlooking Gleann Fhiodhaig are grassy.

The finest feature of Moruisg is the west face of Sgurr nan Ceanraichean, called Creag an Ardachaidh, above the Allt a'Chonais Glen. It is very precipitous and is cleaved by two gullies, which have been climbed (more or less, see Rock Climbs, Appendix II).

Moruisg can be climbed easily from Glen Carron from any convenient point, possibly best from the north-east end of Loch Sgamhain.

Paths

Glen Strathfarrar to Dornie: The former right-of-way path from Strathfarrar to Dornie *via* Patt Lodge on Loch Monar and Iron Lodge in Glen Elchaig is now trackless in that section between the Monar Dam (p. 110) and Patt Lodge, something in excess of 6 miles. The remainder is shown on the map. It seems from the map that a much shorter alternative, which also involves 2 miles less trackless walking, could be had by going west up the Uisge Misgeach road and track from Inchvuilt to the summit of Gleann Innis an Loichel (Clach Daimh). From thence the trackless (and bridgeless) section is only about 4 miles, below the northern corries of An Riabhachan, to the col of An Cruachan. The old track thereafter can be gained beside the

Allt Coire nan Each. This route, however, would have the disadvantage of a pass-height of *c.* 1700 ft. as against the old route's 1450 ft., and the bad section would be at a high level.

Another possibility would seem to be to reach Patt Lodge from the Uisge Misgeach *via* the branch path to the col west of Beinn Dubh an Iaruinn thus cutting the corner of Loch Monar. The Allt Riabhachain could be difficult to cross in flood.

Any route in this area takes one through remote and desolate country and should not be undertaken without due consideration.

Strathcarron Station to Glen Strathfarrar: Another former right-of-way leads from Achintee to Bendronaig Lodge (see p. 114) and from there to Loch Monar by way of the Bealach an Sgoltaidh. The old path which served the former Strathmore Lodge at the west end of the natural Loch Monar has been submerged with it, but according to the one-inch map a new track exists for at least part of the way along the north side of reservoir. The writer has not walked that section since the raising of the water so must be pardoned if he has his suspicions. Nevertheless it is the only route for cross-country excursionists to take, as the alternative by way of Loch Calavie and Patt Lodge is dreary and certainly trackless from Patt onwards to the dam. Despite these difficulties this route, if continued down Glen Strathfarrar, must be one of the finest of its kind in the Highlands.

Place names and their meanings

The following list contains a selection of the more important place-names mentioned in the book, the spellings being those given in the latest edition of the Ordnance Survey maps. The meanings of the names are those given in the previous edition of the Western Highlands District Guide, from which the list has been abstracted in full.

In general, 'Bh' or 'Mh' equals 'V' while 'Fh' is silent as is 'dh' and 'th'. 'S' after an t' is silent.

The present author is no Gaelic scholar. The suggested pronunciation, in brackets, is based on local usage.

A' Chràlaig: (*should be* A' Chràileag), the circular place (*Chrawley*).
A' Ghlas-bheinn: the green mountain.
Allt a' Ghlomaich: the stream of the gloomy hollow or chasm.
Am Bàthaich: the byre (bay).
An Diollaid: the saddle.
An Eag: the notch.
An Leth-Chreag: the half rock.
An Riabhachan: the brindled hill.
An t-Slat-bheinn: the wand mountain.
An Socach: the snout.
An Stac: the stack.
Aonach air Chrith: the shaking height.
Aonach Meadhoin: the middle height (*vane*).
Aonach Sgoilte: the split height (*sgoiltsh*).

Bealach Bhearnais: the pass of the gap.
Bealach Coire Sgoir-adail: (*should be* Sgoradail), the pass of the corrie of the sharp peak.
Bealach Duibh Leac: the pass of the black flagstones.
Bealach an Fhìona: the pass of the wine.
Bealach an t-Sealgaire: the pass of the hunter.
Bealach an Sgàirne: the pass of rumbling.
Bealach an Sgoltaidh: the pass of the splitting.
Ben Aden: the mountain of the face.

Beinn a' Bha' ach Ard: the mountain of the high byre (?).
Beinn Fhada: (*should be* A' Beinn Fhada), the long mountain (*atta*).
Beinn Fhoinnlaidh: Findlay's mountain.
Beinn Gharbh: the rough mountain.
Ben Hiant: (*i.e.* Beinn Shianta), the holy mountain.
Beinn Mheadhoin: the middle mountain.
Beinn na Muice: the mountain of the pig.
Beinn Odhar Bheag: the little dun mountain (*ower veg*).
Beinn Odhar Mhòr: the big dun mountain.
Ben Resipol: *doubtful* (pol = O.N., ból, bólstaðr, a homestead).
Beinn na Seilg: (*should be* Beinn na Seilge), the mountain of hunting.
Ben Sgritheall: *doubtful* (*screel*).
Ben Tee: the mountain of the fairy hillock.
Beinn Tharsuinn: (*should be* Beinn Tarsuinn), the cross mountain.
Beinn an Tuim: the mountain of the hillock.
Bidean a' Choire Sheasgaich: the little peak of the reedy corrie.
Bidean an Eòin Deirg: the little peak of the red bird.
Bràigh a' Choire Bhig: the top of the little corrie.

Càrn an Daimh Bhàin: the cairn of the white stag.
Càrn Eige: the cairn of the notch.
Càrn nam Fiaclan: the cairn of the teeth.
Càrn Ghluasaid: the cairn of moving (*ghlushat*).
Càrn nan Gobhar: the cairn of the goats. (*gower*).
Ceum na h-Aon-choise: the step for one foot.
Ciste Dhubh: the black chest (*kistehoo*).
Coire nan Dearcag: the corrie of the berries (*yercag*).
Coire Dhorrcail: (Coire Thorcuill?), Torquil's corrie (*horcal*).
Coire Domhain: the deep corrie (*don*).
Coire an Iubhair: the corrie of the yew tree (*yewver*).
Creach Bheinn: *probably* the denuded peak (creachan = the bare windswept
 top of hill).
Creag a' Chaoruinn: the rock of the rowan tree.
Creag a' Choir' Aird: the rock of the high corrie.
Creag nan Clachan Geala: the rock of the white stones.
Creag nan Damh: the rock of the stag.
Creag Dhubh: the black rock.
Creag na h-Eige: the rock of the notch.
Creag Ghlas: the grey rock.
Creag Ghorm a' Bhealaich: the blue rock of the pass.
Creag a' Mhàim: the breast rock.
Creag Ruadh: the red rock.
Creag Toll a' Choin: the rock of the dog's den.
Culvain – *see* Gulvain.

Druim Chòsaidh: the ridge with nooks or crevices (*hosey*).
Druim Fiaclach: the toothed ridge.
Druim Shionnach: the ridge of the foxes.

Faochag: the whelk.
Fàradh Nighean Fhearchair: the ladder of Farquhar's daughter (*nine*).
Fuar-tholl Mòr: the big cold hole.

Gairich: the peak of yelling.
Garbh Bheinn: the rough mountain.
Garbh-chàrn: the rough cairn.
Garbh Chìoch Bheag: the little rough pap.
Garbh Chìoch Mhòr: the big rough pap.
Garbh Choire Beag: the little rough corrie.
Garbh Choire Mòr: the big rough corrie.
Gleouraich: uproar.
Gulvain or Gaor Bheinn: thrill mountain (?). O.S. now give Culvain
    (Cul Bhienn) – back shaped mountain.
Gurr Thionail: the peak of the gathering.

Ladhar Bheinn: the forked mountain (*La'arven*).
Loch Beoraid: the beaver loch (?).
Lochan nam Breac: the little loch of the trout.
Luinne Bheinn: *doubtful.*
Lurg Mhòr: the big shank.

Màm na Cloich' Airde: (*should be* Mam na Clochairde), the rounded hill
    of the stony height.
Mam Sodhail: (*should be* Mam Sabhal), the rounded hill of barns. (*Sowl*)
Maol Chinn-dearg: (*should be* Maol Cheann-dearg), the bald red-headed
    hill.
Maoile Lunndaidh: the hill of the boggy place.
Maol Odhar: the dun bald hill (*ower*).
Meall a' Bhealaich: the lump of the pass.
Meall Buidhe: the yellow lump (*booy*).
Meallan Buidhe: the little yellow lump.
Meall a' Chreagain Duibh: the lump of the little black rock.
Meal Dearg Choire nam Muc: the lump of the red corrie of the swine.
Meall Mòr: the big lump.
Meall an Tàrmachain: the lump of the ptarmigan.
Meall na Teanga: the lump of the tongue (*changa*).
Meallan nan Uan: the little lump of the lambs.
Meall an Uillt Chaoil: the lump of the narrow burn.
Moruisg: *doubtful.*
Morvern: the sea gap (a' Mhorbhairn(e) – old name for Loch Sunart).
Morvich: the sea plain.
Mullach Fraoch-choire: the top of the heather corrie.

Plaide Mhòr: the big flat.

Rois-bheinn: (*almost certainly* Froisbheinn), the mountain of the showers.
Rudha na Spréidhe: the point of the herd (*spray*).

Saddle, The: An Dìollaid.
Sàileag: the little heel.
Saoiter Mòr: the big soldier (?).
Sgùman Còinntich: the mossy stack (*sgooman*).
Sgùrr na h-Aide: the peak of the hat (*sgoor na h'Atch*).
Sgùrr Àiridh na Beinne: the peak of the shieling by the peak (*arry*).
Sgùrr na Bà Glaise: the peak of the grey cow.
Sgùrr Beag: the little peak.
Sgùrr a' Bhèalaich Dheirg: the peak of the red gap.
Sgùrr na Càrnach: the peak of the stony place.
Sgùrr nan Ceannaichean: the peak of the merchants.
Sgùrr nan Ceathreamhnan: (*should be* Ceathramhnan), the peak of the quarters (*Cerranan*).
Sgùrr a' Chaorachain: the peak of the white, boiling, tumbling torrent.
Sgùrr a' Chlaidheimh: the peak of the sword (*cleeve*).
Sgùrr Choinnich: the mossy peak.
Sgùrr na Cìche: the pap-shaped peak.
Sgùrr na Ciste Duibhe: the peak of the black chest (*kiste dooy*).
Sgùrr nan Clachan Geala: the peak of the white stones.
Sgùrr à Choire-bheithe: the peak of the birch corrie (*vey*).
Sgùrr Coire Chòinnichean: the peak of the mossy corrie.
Sgùrr nan Coireachan: the peak of the corries.
Sgùrr Coire na Feinne: the peak of the corrie of the warrior band.
Sgùrr a' Choire Ghairbh: the peak of the rough corrie.
Sgùrr a' Choire Ghlais: the peak of the green corrie.
Sgùrr a' Choire-rainich: the peak of the dripping, or bracken, corrie.
Sgùrr nan Conbhairean: the peak of the dog-men.
Sgùrr na Creige: the peak of the rock.
Sgùrr Domhnuill: Donald's peak.
Sgòr na Dìollaid: the peak of the saddle.
Sgùrr an Doire Leathain: the peak of the broad thicket.
Sgùrr a' Dubhdhoire: the peak of the black copse.
Sgùrr na h-Eanchainne: the peak of the brains.
Sgùrr nan Eugallt: the peak of the death precipices (?).
Sgùrr na Fearstaig: (*should be* Sgùrr nam Feartag), the peak of the sea pinks.
Sgùrr an Fhuarail: the peak of the cold place (*ooral*).
Sgùrr an Fhuarain: *doubtful* (*oorain*)
Sgùrr Fhuaran: *doubtful*
Sgùrr Fhuar-thuill: the peak of the cold hole.
Sgùrr na Forcan: the forked peak.
Sgùrr a' Gharg Gharaidh: the peak of the rough den.
Sgùrr Ghiubhsachain: the peak of the fir wood (*goosachan*).
Sgùrr a' Ghlas Leathaid: the peak of the grey hillside (*le'ad*).
Sgùrr na Làpaich: the peak of the bog.
Sgùrr Leac nan Each: the peak of the flat rock of the horses.
Sgùrr an Lochain: the peak of the little loch.
Sgùrr a' Mhaoraich: the peak of the shell-fish.

Sgòr Mhic Eacharna: MacEchern's peak.
Sgùrr a' Mhuilinn: the peak of the mill (*voolin*).
Sgùrr Mòr: the great peak.
Sgùrr na Mòraich: the peak of the sea plain.
Sgùrr na Muice: the peak of the pig.
Sgùrr Nid na h-Iolaire: the peak of the eagle's nest.
Sgùrr Rainich: (*should be* Ronnaich), the dripping peak.
Sgùrr na Ruaidhe: the peak of the red (hind or cow).
Sgùrr nan Saighead: the peak of the arrows (*sight, approx*).
Sgùrr an t-Searraich: the peak of the foal.
Sgùrr Sgiath Àiridh: (*probably* Sgitharigh), the peak of Skiði's shieling
    (*skee'ary*).
Sgùrr na Sgine: the peak of the knife (*sgeen*).
Sgùrr nan Spainteach: the peak of the Spaniards.
Sgùrr Thuilm: the peak of the holm (*hoolm*).
Sgùrr an Utha: the peak of the udder.
Sìthean na Raplaich: the fairy hill of the screes.
Spidean Dhomhuill Bhric: speckled Donald's pinnacle.
Spidean Mialach: the pinnacle of wild animals, *e.g.* hares.
Sròn a' Choire Ghairbh: the nose of the rough corrie.
Sròn Gharbh: the rough nose.
Sròn a' Gharbh Choire Bhig: the nose of the little rough corrie.
Stob a' Chearcaill: the spike of the circle (*heercal*).
Stob Coire nan Cearc: the spike of the hens' corrie, *i.e.* grouse.
Stob a' Choire Odhair: the spike of the dun corrie (*ower*).
Streap: climbing.
Streap Comhlaidh: climbing (adjoining?).
Stùc Bheag: the little peak.
Stùc Mòr: the big peak.

Tigh Mòr na Seilge: the big house of the hunting.
Toll Creagach: the rocky hole.
Tom a' Chòinich: (*should be* Tom Chóinnich), the mossy hillock.

Uisge Misgeach: the water of intoxication (*oosgy misgy*).

Rock Climbs

A Rock-Climber's Guide to the area covered by this District Guide is in course of compilation. As it will be some time before this can be published interim notes on the rock-climbs of the 'Western' district are given below.

MORVERN

There is no record of climbs from any of the hills of this district. On the road between Loch Aline and Drimnin a weathered-out basalt dyke, about 30 ft. high provides routes of all degrees of difficulty for climbers of all ages.

ARDGOUR AND SUNART

Garbh Bheinn

This is the main area for rock-climbing in the district covered by this guide. The many routes on the hill are fully described in the S.M.C. Rock-Climbers' Guide to Glencoe and Ardgour, Vol. 2 – *Glencoe, Beinn Trilleachan and Garbh Bheinn* to which the intending rock-climber is referred. Two of the classic routes are detailed below, as an introduction to the climbs on the mountain.

The rocks of Garbh Bheinn buttress the north and east faces of the mountain above Coir' an Iubhair and are in part set back from that glen above a subsidiary embayment – Garbh Choire Mor. At the head of the latter is the bealach between Garbh Bheinn and Sron a' Garbh Choire Bhig. The general layout of the crags is shown in the photos nos. 8 and 9.

The Great Ridge (1000 ft. in all, Difficult). – The best climbing on the Ridge starts some way up from the bottom, above the upper of two grassy rakes which are prominent features of the face. Above this point the rocks rise in a sharp prow, quite steeply to start with but gradually lying back higher up. To reach the prow two routes can be taken: (a) From near the bottom of the Great Gully climb to the rakes by steep slabby rocks and grass, (b) Follow up the corrie to the left below the steep slabs until a well-marked slanting gully is reached some way from the toe of the buttress. Climb the gully until one can break out easily on the right above the slabby section of the buttress thence traverse slightly downwards to the foot of the prow. The foot of the introductory gully can of course be easily reached from the col if one is approaching from the Glen Tarbert side.

The ridge offers fine climbing of its standard and is very well varied, with arêtes, walls and chimneys, all plentifully supplied with holds and belays.

J. H. Bell and W. Brown, April 1817

Great Gully (*900 ft., Very Difficult*). – The full length of the gully is 1200 ft., but the lower 300 ft. are uninteresting and the best route of approach goes up the rocks on the north flank. Traverse in when the gully deepens.

After one high easy pitch the gully widens and is divided by a 100-ft. rib. The left fork starts with an overhang and while this has been climbed, it is very hard so the normal route as classified above goes 30 ft. up the rib and traverses right into the right-hand chimney. This is climbed for 70 ft. to a saddle and a traverse is then made back over the central rib to the left fork. A stretch of easy climbing follows up the Great Cave, which is the crux. Here the route goes up the right wall. Start approximately 60 ft. out from the cave. Surmount the initial overhang by a flake-hold. Move up to the right past a bulge, then climb up parallel to the gully by slabs and grooves. Finish up a short wall 1 yard to the left of the gully bed. (This whole pitch requires a run out of 100 ft.)

Beyond is a hard pitch of 40 ft., then by easy climbing to the fork of the gully, which is 150 ft., from the top. The right fork is the less direct and looks easy, while the left fork ends in a repellant chimney, so the normal route goes by the buttress between the two forks. Start near its right-hand side and follow the only line of weakness. A third of the way up make an exposed 30-ft. traverse round a nose to the left. Beyond there is clean rough rock all the way to the top.

W. H. Murray and D. Scott, June 1946.

ARDNAMURCHAN

Unfortunately there are few large cliffs in Ardnamurchan, but many of the numerous small crags provide short, sporting routes (see photo, no. 14). It is well worth carrying a rope while exploring the district so that these climbs can be tackled for practice. The only sizeable cliffs so far discovered are on Beinn na Seilg and these have genuine rock-climbs of some merit. The cliff was explored on 17th April, 1949, by R. E. Chapman and G. Francis.

Beinn na Seilg

Viewed from the west the cliff is divided into 2 masses by an area of easy scrambling – the Central Break (B). To the south of it, Hebrides Wall (C) stretches to the south-west Buttress. This Wall narrows at its centre to Gabbro Slab, which provides an easy way to the summit. To the north of Central Break lies Cuillin Buttress (A) (see diagram below). The rock is gabbro.

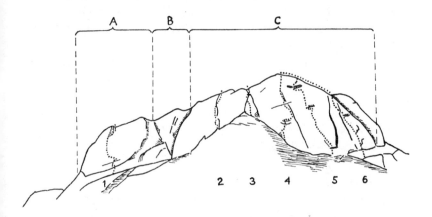

South-West Buttress (Moderate). – This forms the right-hand boundary of Hebrides. The best route stays close above the Wall from the start to the summit. *Diag. route 6.*

Faradh Dubh (165 ft., Very Difficult). – Start below the prominent crack on the right side of the Wall.

1: 60 ft. From a small ledge near the bottom of the crack move steeply up to the left. Small belay. 2: 60 ft. Straight up two bulges, turn the left-hand one and continue to a small over-hang. 3: 30 ft. Traverse left until the overhang can be climbed, then up to the right. Thread belay. 4: 15 ft. Easy rocks lead to the crest of the South-West Buttress. *Diag. route 5.*

Trident Climb (125 ft., Very Difficult). – Start at three prongs of rock between Faradh Dubh and Gabbro Slab.

1: 35 ft. Up the prongs. From a shaky spike above make a big stride to the right. Gain a roomy ledge by a mantleshelf move. Belay on left. 2: 50 ft. Traverse right to a small crack. Follow it for 8 ft., then turn a small overhang on the left. Block belay. 3: 35 ft. A choice of routes leads to easy ground. *Diag. route 4.*

Gabbro Slab (50 ft., Moderate). – Start from the highest ground at the foot of Hebrides Wall. Up the slab above, keeping to the left. Various belays. Easy rocks lead on. *Diag. route 2.*

Geologist's Groove (100 ft., Difficult). – Start half-way between Gabbro Slab and the Central Break.

1: 40 ft. Up a heather-filled crack until it overhangs. An excursion is made to the left, and back to a wide bay. Belay. 2: 60 ft. Onwards by the direct continuation of the crack, thence by easier rocks to the top. *Diag. route 2.*

Sunset Wall (145 ft., Very Difficult). – Start on the grass terrace below Cuillin Buttress half-way between the Central Break and a large rock step. (Cairn).

1: 65 ft. Up inclined ledges to a grass platform. 2: 55 ft. Traverse left, then up steep rocks to a pulpit. 3: 25 ft. Up a slab on the right. Belay above, left. *Diag. route 1.*

MOIDART

Although there is a superabundance of steep, craggy slopes in Moidart, there appears to be few buttresses of any size. Above Loch Shiel, however, there are some large rock masses on the slopes of the Beinn Odhars which have given a good climb. All the hills should give good winter excursions if adequate snow conditions obtain but as they are near the seaboard, good snow for climbing is not often found.

Beinn Odhar Mhor: Shiel Buttress.

This buttress, on the lower slopes of the mountain overlooking Loch Shiel, forms part of the narrow ridge sweeping down in a south-easterly direction from Sgurr an Iubhair (O.S. NM 859780). The rock is extraordinarily compact and reliable. The buttress is about 400 ft. high and is well seen in profile from the road just east of Glenfinnan. On this occasion an approach was made along the shore of the loch. This proved very time-consuming due to heavy undergrowth and difficulties of access at the start. Future visitors would be well-advised to cross over the mountain from the pass between Lochs Shiel and Eilt. As mentioned in the General section of the Guide, the slopes of the Beinn Odhars offer plenty of scope for exploration, which should be rewarding if the quality of the rock elsewhere is as high as on Shiel Buttress.

The Rising (*370 ft., Severe*). – The front of the buttress is divided by a dark overhung recess high up. Start at the lowest rocks of the left-hand section. Climb to a wide ledge where the buttress steepens (150 ft.). Climb up right then back left up steep shelf to small stance below overhangs (70 ft.). An old abseil sling was found here. Climb by grooves and cracks above to the top (150 ft.).

R. Campbell & A. W. Ewing, May 1969

LOCHEIL AND MORAR, LOCH ARKAIG AND GLEN DESSARRY

No rock-climbs of any merit are known and none are likely to be found. Easy scrambles can be had on slabby rocks on Coire Chaisil of Sgurr Thuilm, but these are less steep than they appear from a distance. Slabby scrambles may also be had on the east side of Stob Coire nan Cearc and on the east side of Druim a' Chuirn, the slabs on the latter being particularly pleasant, but not very continuous.

Just east of the watershed in Glen Pean, on the north side of the valley, there is a large pinnacle reminiscent of the Pillar Rock, about half-scale. The local name for this feature is, in fact, The Pillar! It is approached by a steep grassy scramble from the glen and is ascended by taking it from the north. The summit boulder is awkward. A rock-climb might be made up the south ridge of the pinnacle. On the watershed of the glen itself landslipped blocks as big as houses lie in a jumbled mass, the tunnels between and beneath them providing some speleological sport for those equipped with torches and rope.

In winter the situation changes, and under average, or better, conditions some good climbing may be had on the hills of these areas. Many of the corries are sufficiently steep to provide sporting routes to the summits, while of the ridges, three merit special mention. The ridge between Stob Coire nan Cearc and Streap can be quite difficult at times, depending on the snow and is not at all simple under average conditions. The section of the Sgurr na Ciche – Sgurr Mor ridge as far east as An Eag requires care in places and is a fine winter excursion. There is no record of an ascent of Fraoch Bheinn by its north ridge, but this is narrow and rocky and should give a sporting route if well snowed up.

GLEN GARRY AND KNOYDART

An Caisteal, Loch Hourn

An Caisteal has a large slabby north face rising from the corrie formed by the neighbouring tops of Carn Mairi and Meall nan Eun. This face attains a height of about 700 ft. with a magnificent central sweep of clean slabs which give excellent Etive-like climbing on sound rock. The wings of the cliff are broken by grass ledges but possibly good climbs could be made here also. The following two climbs take the central sweep. Pegs for belays as required.

Battlement Slab, 640 ft. (Very Severe). – Start below and right of the toe of the central sweep at a brown slab capped by overhang (arrow). Climb easy rocks rightwards then traverse left delicately to ledge (50 ft.). Take watercourse groove above to large grass ledge (50 ft.). Up to large ledge below impressive slabby scoop (40 ft.). Climb scoop trending left for about 40 ft. Move up rightwards until a delicate step enables one to reach a block. Climb smooth greasy corner above (peg) to nose and go back to flake belay (80 ft.). Take curving crack above and pull round block overhang on to grass (60 ft.). Walk up to broken corner which trends slightly left towards centre of big sweep of slabs (50 ft.). Now take impressive corner ramp which sweeps up left to small stance (110 ft.). Move left across slab and go up corner on good holds. Pull out left past overhanging grass then up easily passing short wall to belay below small overhang (80 ft.). Go left across short walls and belay under steep corner (40 ft.). Ascend the corner and lay away round overhanging block, traverse left on obvious line to finish up small ramp (80 ft.).

D. S. Nicol & P. Gunn, 22nd June 1967

Portcullis (675 ft., Very Severe). – Follows a fairly direct line up the left edge of the central sweep of clean slabs except for a grassy leftwards divergence, an escape made necessary by bad weather conditions, near the top.

Start about 50 ft. left of Battlement Slab. Climb short steep crack to rowan and up groove to thread belay on ledge under overhangs (35 ft.). Move right and through break in overhang whence groove

50. On the Mam Sodhail – Carn Eige Ridge. Note the large cairn on Mam Sodhail.

51. Sgurr na Lapaich (Glen Cannich) and An Riabhachan, from Sron Garbh (Glen Affric).

52. The summit ridge of An Riabhachan.

53. The West Monar and Achnashellach Hills from Beinn Eighe. Sgurr nan Ceathreamhnan (right), Bidean a'Choire Sheasgaich and Lurg Mhor (centre) an the Bidean an Eoin Dearg group (left).

54. The Monar Dam.

55. Sguman Coinntich from Loch Long. Ben Killilan on left.

leads to grass basin. Climb clean slab directly above to grass tuft and traverse left to grass ledge (70 ft.). Climb delicately up slab, slightly right, then left beneath overlap, to break (peg). Delicately up right to small ledge, place another peg runner a few feet above and move left to climb groove to grass ledge and peg belay (70 ft., crux). Traverse right a few feet then follow line of pock marks and quartz knobs, moving right finally to gain ledge at foot of prominent groove (50 ft.). Climb groove to small grass ledge and belays (40 ft.). Climb thin crack directly above bulge to grass and go up to below left hand of two short grooves (50 ft.). Go up left 30 ft., rightwards a few feet on narrow grass gangway, then climb to ledge under prominent band of pink rock and belay beneath recess (80 ft.). Go round right over large perched blocks to climb overhanging niche, then up left to grass ledge above start. Climb a further 40 ft. directly above by flake and short groove to another ledge (80 ft.). Steep rocks continue above but were avoided by following grassy grooves and ramps leftwards to gain top in a further 200 ft.

I. S. Clough and B. Rex, 22nd July, 1967

Meall nan Eun, Loch Hourn

On the left hand side of the coire formed by Carn Mairi, An Caisteal and Meall nan Eun (on the slopes of Meall nan Eun) is a line of crags, more broken than those of An Caisteal. From right to left are a rocky cone-shaped hummock, two buttresses slightly set back in a bay and, left again, a big buttress consisting of numerous rock ribs which culminate in a big slab. All these are separated by grassy gullies. The following climb lies on the right-hand of the two buttresses set in the bay.

Round House (480 ft., Mild Severe). – Climb centre of steep slab to grass ledge (120 ft.). Traverse right to good rocks right of grass gully then left across gully to large grass ledge (120 ft.). Continue directly to belay on another grass ledge (120 ft.) then more easily to top.

G. A. White & J. A. Gillcrest, 22nd June, 1967

Ladhar Bheinn

Coire na Cabaig. – This is the loftier side corrie adjoining Coire Dhorrcail and separated from it by Stob Dhorrcail – a snub-nosed bastion of 500 ft., which should offer an easy if uninteresting scramble up its frontal face, or scope for shorter and harder climbs in the gullies on its flanks.

The main feature of the corrie, however, is the sheer-looking 800 ft.

north-west face of Stob a' Chearchaill which forms its east wall. From Arnisdale it remotely resembles the Grandes Jorasses. This is not confirmed, for although everywhere steep and well delineated with gullies and chimneys, it is too well vegetated for continuous rock climbs. In winter, however, it promises at least half a dozen distinctive routes.

Gaberlunzie (First Winter Ascent. 800 ft.). – The main Central Gully, a deep trough in the middle of the face leading up to a small notch on the serrated summit ridge of Stob a' Chearchaill. It is as a winter route that it deserves attention, and is the only recorded climb on these cliffs.

Above a small snow fan the lower 200 ft. of the gully is steep, and gives 100 ft. of hard climbing up to a snow channel which steepens to a large cave beneath a chockstone at 180 ft. This was overcome with difficulty on the left. Then the angle eases and there are no major difficulties until 200 ft. from the top, where the walls again converge, and the gully becomes a shallow ice runnel. The last 60 ft. of climbing up the right hand enclosing gully wall were perhaps the hardest on the climb.

A. G. Nicol, R. W. P. Barclay & T. W. Patey, 14th April, 1963. Three hours in good conditions.

Coire Dhorrcail. – The cliffs at the head of this corrie are the finest feature on the mountain. At the back of the corrie the crags attain their greatest height at the Spider Buttress, all of 1200 ft. in height and characterized by a central snowfield reminiscent of the 'White Spider'. The right and left enclosing ribs on either side of the snowfield should be climbable, and might even repay investigation in summer.

In the centre of the cirque the most obvious straight snow gully with a single chockstone pitch at mid height is the gully climbed by Raeburn and his companions in 1898. Its right hand border is a very well-defined square-cut oblong rib of some 500–600 ft., as yet unclimbed. Between Raeburn's Gully (which has an alternative untried left hand variant) and the Spider Buttress there is a long narrow gully with successive concealed ice-pitches which scores the full height of the cliffs and lies well back in the angle where the Spider Buttress abuts upon the main line of crags. It seemed to be the most elegant line in the corrie on a first acquaintance, and, in fact, yielded a fast, exhilarating climb described below.

Viking Gully (First Winter Ascent. 1200 ft.). – The true first pitch was avoided by a slanting snow rake on the left because of falling ice. The rake entered the gully below a narrow snow funnel. Another ice pitch and a long snow trough led to a narrow twisting channel leading into the recessed upper portion of the gully. For the next 400 ft. there was a series of abrupt ice pitches 50–60 ft. in height. Finally, 300 ft. from the top a long snow fan led to a (possibly corniced) exit into a well-defined col between two small peaks of equal height on the main ridge.

Discounting the exceptionally favourable conditions on the first ascent, the route compares with the classic Crowberry Gully on the Buachaille, and can be thoroughly recommended as a winter climb. *A. G. Nicol, R.W.P. Barclay and T. W. Patey, 15th April, 1963.* Two hours in good conditions.

As noted in the District account these climbs were made during unusually hard conditions. Previous and subsequent summer visitors agree that the rock-climbing potential is not good.

Gairich

The east ridge of Gairich has a short rocky section which might prove interesting in winter.

GLEN MORISTON, GLEN SHIEL AND GLENELG

Druim Shionnach (Aonach air Chrith)

A climb has been made on the rocks of the west face of Druim Shionnach. This is reached by walking up the ridge bounding Coir' an t-Slugain on the east until the 2800 ft. contour is reached and traversing right to the foot of the crag. The following description is abridged from the *Fell and Rock C.C. Journal*.

The Silver Slab (Just Severe in rubbers). – Between a large gully in the centre of the crag and 2 large caves on the left there lie two buttresses separated by a smaller gully. In the centre of the left-hand one of these a small chimney rises, petering out after 50 ft. The climb starts on the face immediately to the left of the chimney. Small cairn left by the original party may not have survived.

1: 80 ft. Straight up by delicate press movements. Traverse right across chimney to a good belay. 2: 70 ft. Straight ahead from belay for 6 ft. then traverse left and continue up on original line until the slab becomes almost holdless above a good ledge. Climb the crack to the left and traverse right on to a good stance and unsatisfactory belay. 3:

60 ft. Take the wall above for 10 ft. and then make a delicate traverse left into a corner. Follow the crack in the corner, the face on the left, rejoin the crack and reach a grass ledge on the edge of the crag (way off). Return to the wall on the right and a shaky belay in 15 ft., best taken in the corner to the left. 4: 50 ft., Straight up, then right, to a pinnacle and belay. After the first 15 ft. the climbing becomes easier. 5: 30 ft. The wall above, traversing right later, leads to the finish.

J. W. Haggas, S. Thompson, Phillis B. White, 1st August, 1938.

The Saddle

The Sgurr na Forcan ridge described in the main section of this Guide gives a good scramble which might be classed as 'easy' under summer conditions, but which is by no means a walk. In winter it can become quite difficult, especially on the steep west side of the peak.

Eastwards from the summit there are slabby rocks on the south side of the ridge above Coire Mhalagain. There is one good climb on these slabs and others, perhaps less interesting, could be made.

Easter Buttress (300 ft., Severe by Direct Route). – On approaching the ridge from Glen Shiel, turn left as soon as the rocks are reached and traverse below the crags, above a dry-stane dyke. The rocks are rather broken at first, but after a short distance they give place to steeper, slabbier masses which do not reach so far down the hillside as do those of the broken section. The slabby rocks are limited on their right by a shallow gully and Easter Buttress, lying between this gully and a series of overhanging slabs further to the left, is quite well defined.

The Buttress gives a good, clean, steep climb which is severe if the crest is followed throughout. Easier climbing, about very difficult in standard, can be had by avoiding the difficulties on the right, above the shallow gully. The climb finishes a few yards before the beginning of the horizontal knife-edge shown on the main ridge.

D. Piggott and G. S. Johnstone, Easter 1961.

Beinn Sgritheall: North Face

North Buttress (Winter Ascent 400 ft., Severe). – Looking up from Loch Bealach na h-Oidhche a big gully splits the north face. To the left is a shallower gully. To the left of this is the North Buttress. The buttress has 3 rock steps separated by grassy ledges. Choose your route. Rock loose, but the steeper the better. The route was repeated the following summer. Difficult. H. M. Brown & A. Dunsire (B.F.M.C.). 20th October, 1965.

H. M. Brown & A. Smith, 14th September, 1964

KINTAIL

The climbing in this area is mainly on flaggy granulites and mica-schists. These flaggy rocks are usually set at a steep angle and present rather smooth, slabby faces to the climber. There is often much vegetation, but nevertheless some fairly good routes are to be found. Many of the climbs are more suited to tricouni nails than to composition soles as the former can make better use of the thin soil-filled fissures which often traverse the slabs. Between Glen Croe and Loch Long much of the rock belongs to the Lewisian Assemblage and provides much better climbing, but like other areas made up of this ancient rock, the crags are small.

Sgurr nan Saighead

EASTERN CLIFFS. The eastern cliffs are approached from Gleann Lichd. One climb has been made up an obvious S-shaped crack which lies at the apex of the left-hand of the 2 *large* scree cones. The start is cairned and arrowed.

California (250 ft., Severe). – The chimney was climbed for about 25 ft. and then the right wall for about 40 ft.; a further 50 ft. of loose stones led to a belay. A much narrower chimney was climbed for 50 ft. and the next 8 ft. (crux) on the wall; a further 70 ft. led to a belay. Fifty ft. of crambling up and leftwards led to grass, by which the party returned to the start.

J. H. Barber and C. A. Simpson (through leads).

NORTH-EAST FACE. – This face of the mountain is composed of irregular rock buttresses divided by several deep, narrow gullies. The Forked Gully is the deep, prominent gully in the centre of the face with a wide scree cone beneath it.

Forked Gully (Winter route). – Climb the gully and after about 150 ft. enter the left-hand fork, which becomes very narrow. The average angle is about 60 degrees. Under the conditions prevailing at the time of the first ascent the gully gave a good climb finishing with a 12-ft. ice pitch.

The right fork of this gully, if filled with snow, would give a good climb.

J. H. Barber and C. A. Simpson, 2nd January, 1957.

Sgurr Fhuaran

NORTH FACE. – An obvious gully splits this face from top to bottom, with a triple fork in the upper reaches. The height of the gully is approximately 700 ft. and it gives a winter climb. On the first ascent three steep snow-ice pitches were climbed (15, 25 and 40 ft.). The centre fork was then followed. A steep, straightforward snow slope led to a vertical exit at the summit.

J. G. Burns and H. Kindness, 2nd January, 1957.

Sgurr na Ciste Duibhe

Solo Gully (350 ft., Winter Climb). – An obvious line on the left side of the corrie between Sgurr na Ciste Duibhe and Sgurr na Spainteach. Climbed in crampons. Straightforward, with two very short ice pitches. Exit to ridge 200 yards from the summit of the latter peak.

J. G. Burns, 3rd January. 1957.

Sgurr na Carnach

The north side of this mountain is very broken, and has one definite gully, leading from the foot of the face to the summit. It is easily recognized, when approached from the north, by its resemblance to a dog's hind leg.

Dog's Leg Gully (550 ft., Winter Climb). – Start in the wide corridor to the left of a prominent rock buttress and climb up for about 100 ft. on easy snow. At this point the gully divides, the right fork continuing up to the western ridge of the mountain and the left fork being blocked by a bluff of rock and small ledges, above which the gully leads straight to the summit. On the first ascent the left-fork was climbed over the bluff which was well-iced and gave some difficulty. The rest of the gully was straight-forward and the climb finished about 10 yards to the west of the summit.

J. H. Barber and G. Burns (through leads), 3rd January, 1957.

Beinn Fhada

There are some fine crags on the north-east face of Sgorr a' Choire Ghairbh. The main face below the summit is rather grassy and disappointing, but some good routes have been made on the smaller buttresses to the south.

Summit Buttress (ca. 450 ft., Difficult). – Start to the right of the rightmost of two gullies containing the apparent summit as seen from the corrie. Dangerous grass-covered slabs are climbed until the rock becomes cleaner. Easy climbing to a salient bulge – prominent on the ascent. Traverse left across the gully to the summit buttress proper and thence straight up.

Not recommended, but might make a good winter climb.

D. Piggott and G. S. Johnstone, Easter 1961.

Right-Hand Gully (450 ft., Winter Climb). – The rightmost of the two cutting Summit Buttress. Stretches of good snow and two pitches of considerable difficulty at the time of the first ascent.

C. L. Donaldson, J. Russell and G. Dutton, 14th April, 1951.

Needle's Eye Buttress (250 ft., 'Difficult with harder pitches'). – The sharply-defined buttress to the left of the Summit Buttress. Named from a square projection, half-way up, which is pierced by a hole.

The general line taken was along the edge. Below the Needle's Eye the pitch was hard and steep and a short traverse was made to the left. A move leftwards under a great cantilever led to a flake and so to the top of the square projection. Above this the climb was at its steepest and thinnest, with one pitch of 35 ft. to a small flake, the next on very small holds over a bulge and up a long flake on the edge, and a third which compelled the leader to descend about 10 ft., across a scoop on plant holds and climb its far side.

R. Grieve and R. Brown, 9th June, 1949.

Left of Needle's Eye Buttress is a broad grassy gully, beyond which is a prominent rib with almost vertical side walls – this is Guide's Rib.

Guide's Rib (310 ft., Very Difficult). – The Rib rises steeply in pitches of 50, 45 and 75 ft. to a large block. A short groove on the right leads to the top of the block. Rib continues for 35 ft. to a level, knife-edged arête and so to a narrow wall, climbed to a gendarme, behind which is a hole through the rib. Climb this direct and finish rib to easy ground.

G. H. Kitchen and R. J. Porter, 12th July, 1955.

Porter's Climb (395 ft., Difficult). – This lies to the left (south) of Guide's Rib where the foot of the cliff is lower. It starts from the left edge of the lowest section.

From a cairn, climb near the left edge of vegetatious slabs in pitches of 70, 85 and 45 ft. to the base of steeper rock. Climb this on the right to the foot of a crack, followed up to a large rocky stance. Easy slabs lead to a corner on the left, climbed to a good ledge. A grassy groove or a difficult slab on the right lead to the top of a small pinnacle and then to easy ground.

Party as above.

Continuation Climb (100 ft., Difficult). – This starts from a grass ledge on the same level as the finish of the last climb, but 20 yards away, across a gully on the right. Step up a few feet and then round to the right on to a steep wall. Climb the wall and continue up easier slabs, with a stance at 15 ft.

Party as above.

The Needle (Severe, by direct ascent of slab). – The climb is not precisely located, but is described as lying a few hundred yards south of Needle's Eye Buttress. It is slabby and culminates in a fine pinnacle.

The route goes up the north edge of the buttress. Starting from the lowest point, climb the groove to the edge of the slab. Traverse right to a rib of porphyry (spike belay) – the direct ascent of the slab is severe. Excellent climbing leads up the rib in pitches of 30, 90 and 65 ft. to a cairn. Traverse up to the right for 30 ft. to a large vibrating flake. Climb wall above for 30 ft. to the top of a pinnacle (this is a magnificent situation). Cross a narrow gap and scramble up to the main ridge.

W. J. Cole, J. R. Marshall and I. Oliver, 20th July, 1952.

There are steep rocks in Coire an Sgairne, the branch corrie to the east of the one containing the crags described above. There are no records of any climbs on them.

The Glen Croe – Loch Long Area

Much of this high tract of country has numerous small bluffs and crags. Several short climbs have been made on these, mainly by local climbers. One major crag, however, looks as though it should provide more serious work. This is Biod an Fhitich on the south side of the valley of the River Glennan, about 1½ miles north-east from Dornie. The cliff must be about 300 ft. in height or more and is steep, although rather vegetated. There are strong rumours that several unrecorded climbs have been made here.

GLEN CANNICH

An Riabhachan: North-East Face

Spindrift Gully. (650 ft., Grade II). – The gully cuts straight up through the right half of prominent rock face lying just west of the Sgurr na Lapaich col. It contains one pitch and is steep in its upper half.

D. Smith & J. G. Stewart, 12th April, 1969.

GLEN STRATHFARRAR, ETC.

See reference to 'Rock Climbs' by R. Frere, 1938 in Bibliography, p. 27.

Maoile Lunndaidh, Creag Toll a' Choin

Mica Ridge (300 ft., Difficult). – From the floor of the corrie rises a steep, continuous, vegetatious cliff on the left. The route is up the first definite ridge to the right of this wall. Keep on the crest or near it. Traverse by steps and ledges on the steep right side, then a lone groove to an exposed corner. Go left to the crest and up it to a knife-edge. On the first ascent there was a snow comb and a big cornice at the top.

A. Watson and A. Watson (Sen.), May 1954.

Moruisg, Creag an Ardachaidh

The two gullies on the western face of the crag have been investigated.

North Gully (Moderate). – Several pitches were avoided by climbing out to the side. *South Gully (Easy).* On the first descent a vertical pitch (? impossible) 100 ft. down, was avoided by the right bank.

R. Frere, K. Robertson and J. Wright, 19th October, 1937.

(E. W. Hodge found the South Gully to be blocked on the ascent by a very large chockstone.)

Sgurr na Fearstaig: Sgurr na Muice

For notes on these crags see *S.M.C.J.*, xx, 153; *C.C.J.*, 1954, p. 53. The climbs do not appear to be of much account.

Sgurr a' Mhuilinn: Creag Ghlas

This did not quite come up to expectations. There are two buttresses: the East Buttress is about 800 ft. high, but ill-defined and grassy; the West Buttress is about 450 ft. high and is steep, compact and slabby. The rock is immaculately sound but poorly provided with holds. Natural belays are almost totally absent.

West Buttress. The Lizard (450 ft., Very Severe). – A prominent rib divides the buttress into smooth slabs on the left and steep walls and grassy corners on the right. The route follows this rib. Climb to broad rock terrace in two pitches, keeping to crest (130 ft. and 70 ft.). Climb enormous slab above in two pitches, keeping close to right edge

(100 ft. and 100 ft.). Walk left up glacis and climb short steep wall to finish (50 ft.).

D. Bathgate & R. N. Campbell, August 1967.

East Buttress (Oh! 800 ft., Mild Very Severe). – The buttress is roughly triangular in shape. This route follows the left bounding edge more or less closely, and starts at slabs immediately right of the gully on the left. Climb slab directly and delicately for 40 ft. and continue up and right of grassy fault to grassy ledge (130 ft.). Easily now to belay below another steep slab (150 ft.). Climb this by thin rightward-sloping crack then go up easier ground beyond (120 ft.). Continue up to belay below steep wall (130 ft.). Climb wall, stepping left after 15 ft. then up to final rocks to belay at large flake below short corner (140 ft.). Climb corner and step out left then up right to finish (130 ft.).

Dr. Patey notes (*S.M.C.J., 1970*) that, 'Unaware of previous visits we, in June 1968, also climbed the left-bounding edge more or less directly. It seemed an obvious choice for a first visit. Although we took a direct line and did not avoid any obstacles, the standard of difficulty encountered was no more than Moderately Difficult. Detailed description seemed pointless because although the rock was good, the pitches were straightforward and lacked variety. Obviously there must be some puzzling error of identification?

'The original Very Severe line was christened *Oh!* The 1968 Difficult line is therefore entitled *Oh Dear!* It did seem to be the natural line as well as the longest, so both routes must be within whispering distance of each other (although presumably not identical?).'

J. Renny & M. Strong, August 1967.

Advice to Hill-Walkers

The Scottish Climbing Clubs consider it desirable to give advice to hill-walkers – especially to those with limited knowledge of conditions in Scotland. The present time is appropriate as an increasing number of people make use of the Scottish mountains in summer and in winter.

The Clubs are constrained to give this advice owing to the accidents in recent years which led to serious injury or death, caused trouble and anxiety to local residents called from their ordinary vocations, and to experienced climbers summoned from long distances to render assistance. Such assistance must not be regarded as always available, and it is only fair and reasonable that local helpers be paid adequately for their assistance.

The guide books issued by the Scottish Mountaineering Club describe routes which range from difficult climbs to what are in fine weather mere walks. It cannot be stressed too strongly that an expedition, which in fine weather is simple, may cease to be so if the weather becomes bad or mist descends In winter, conditions on the hills change – what in summer is a walk may become a mountaineering expedition.

In many cases accidents are caused by a combination of events, no one of which singly would have been serious. Ample time should be allowed for expeditions, especially when the route is unknown. Further, before setting out on an expedition, parties should leave information as to their objectives and route and, without exception, have the courage to turn back when prudence so dictates.

In expeditions of any magnitude a party should consist of not less than three members, and they should never separate. If the party is large, two of the experienced members should bring up the rear.

If 1 member of the party is injured, another member should stay with him with all available food and spare clothing, while the remainder go to secure help. Great care should be taken in marking the spot where the injured man is left. Unless a conspicuous landmark is chosen, for example the junction of two streams, it is difficult to locate the spot, especially if the return is from a different direction or by night.

Some common causes of difficulty are:

Underestimate of time required for expedition.

Slow or untried companions or members who are in poor training.

Illness caused through unwise eating or drinking.

Extreme cold or exhaustion through severe conditions.

Poor, soft snow; steep hard snow; snowstorms; mist.

Change in temperature rapidly converting soft snow into ice – involving step cutting.

Rain making rock slippery or snow filling the holds when rock climbing.

Frost after snow or rain glazing rocks with ice.

Sudden spates rendering the crossing of burns dangerous or impossible and necessitating long detours.

Hints – Equipment:

All parties should carry:

Simple First Aid equipment, torch, whistle, watch, one-inch O.S. map, compass, and be able to use them.

Except in a few spots in Skye* where the rocks are magnetic, the compass direction is certain to be correct even if it differs from one's sense of direction.

Ice axes should be carried if there is any chance of snow or ice, and a rope unless it is certain not to be required.

Clothing: At all times reserve clothing should be carried. Temperatures change rapidly, especially at high levels. Clothing should be warm; in winter a Balaclava helmet and thick woollen gloves should be carried. Well-shod boots should always be worn.

Food: Each member of a party should carry his own food. Climbers will find from experience what kind of food suits their individual need. Normally, jams and sugar are better than meat as more rapidly

---

*Also a few places in Rhum and Mull and see p. 64 of this District Guide (*Author, Western Highlands*).

converted into energy. Most people will find it advisable to avoid alcohol on the hills, but a flask may be carried for emergencies. Light meals at frequent intervals are better than heavy meals at long intervals. In winter it may be advisable to make an early stop for food if shelter is found.

It is essential at all times to respect proprietary and sporting rights, especially during the shooting season, and to avoid disturbing game in deer forests and on grouse moors.

Issued with the authority of

Scottish Mountaineering Club
Dundee Rambling Club
Ladies' Scottish Climbing Club
Moray Mountaineering Club.
Creagh Dhu Mountaineering Club
Edinburgh University Mountaineering Club
Cairngorm Club
Grampian Club
Lomond Mountaineering Club
Lomond Mountaineering Club of Scotland
Etchachan Club

INDEX